Praise for *fro*

Pay attention to the strategies outlined by Margit. As an attention expert, I always say "be intentional with your attention." Margit gives you the tools you need to pay attention and make the changes you seek; she outlines a clear roadmap and provides practical exercises you can apply immediately. Enjoy her process of notice, exhale, and redirect.

> **–Neen James,** author of *Attention Pays* and *Folding Time*

From Hope to Habit is a revelation for anyone on a quest to turn resolutions into reality. Margit brilliantly combines her clinical expertise with real-life examples, easy exercises, and chapter recaps that empower readers to develop healthy and sustainable habits. As a trusted guide, Margit has created a practical road map that ensures that YOU are always the one in the driver's seat of your own success.

> **–Aimee Cohen,** author of *Woman Up!: Overcoming the 7 Deadly Sins that Sabotage Your Success*

From Hope to Habit gives readers science-based instruction for creating sustainable positive habits. If you are longing to truly change, you have a chance to learn solutions from an expert. Benefit and thrive because Margit Cox Henderson's thirty years as a therapist have taught her what it takes to live your best intentions.

> **–Elizabeth McCormick,** former US Army Black Hawk Helicopter Pilot and author of *The P.I.L.O.T. Method*

In *From Hope to Habit*, Dr. Margit Henderson offers a reusable framework for making good habits, well, a habit. In my work helping organizations avoid cyber risk, strong habits are the difference between security and disaster. Don't just hope for change, buy this book, implement the actionable solutions and vastly improve your health, wealth and relationships.

–**John Sileo,** author of *Privacy Means Profit: Prevent Identity Theft and Secure You and Your Bottom Line*

In a comprehensive yet manageable manner, *From Hope to Habit* readers can experience and live their best intentions. You will be guided by the Dr. Henderson's authentic journey, be provided spaces and time to reflect your thoughts and actions, and be encouraged with challenges, action-steps, and humor.

–**Terri Davis,** Ph.D., Director of the Psy.D. Program at the University of Denver's Graduate School of Professional Psychology

Holy smokes! I just finished Margit Henderson's new book, from *From Hope to Habit*, and am blown away by the transformational process she has created, full of easily-accessible, boots-on-the-ground hacks to turn good intentions into lived realities. What do I love most? She doesn't prescribe a one-size-fits-all template, but encourages the reader to align the exercises with their own strengths and personalities. From the micro-resolution to the When-Then Action Plan Recap, Margit presents her wisdom in a warm, authentic, and compassionate way, teaching us all how to shine a little brighter.

–**Lisa Foster,** developer of the *Shine from Your Original Design* program

Margit Cox Henderson's new book, *From Hope to Habit*, is a brilliant, unique guide to changing habits. Knowing we need to change a habit is one thing, but actually making a new habit happen is another. Henderson shows us how to take micro-steps to accomplish any type of new habit. A must-read for anybody wanting to make a change.

–**Janice Litvin,** author of *Banish Burnout Toolkit*

I so appreciate Margit Henderson's new book *From Hope to Habit.* None of us would think of taking off on a long, complex journey with many stops and starts without a detailed plan. Yet as humans we often make resolutions and promises to ourselves in a second without any thought of how we might actually accomplish this goal or desire. Margit shares her own stories with authenticity and vulnerability, which inspires us to make our own changes. More importantly she provides a detailed roadmap, a process to establish good intentions and turn those intentions into regular habits. I'm definitely inspired.

–**Katharine Halpin,** author of *Alignment for Success: Bringing out the Best in Yourself, Your Teams and Your Company*

Margit is incredibly experienced and shows her talents for teaching in this book. She presents the theory and then masterfully shows the reader how to immediately integrate the theory in bite-sized pieces. A must read for anyone serious about self-improvement!

–**Cynthia Stadd Orvis,** developer of the *End Your Food War: Reclaim Your Weight, Health and Peace* and *Food Relationship Reset* programs

from HOPE *to* HABIT

**Science-Based Solutions to
Live Your Best Intentions**

Margit Cox Henderson, Ph.D.

From Hope to Habit:
Science-Based Solutions to Live Your Best Intentions
by Margit Cox Henderson, Ph.D.

The only true stories in these pages are those describing my life. The other characters, whose challenges and triumphs are described herein, are completely fictional. Any similarity to someone you know is coincidental yet speaks to how universal these issues are.

Books may be purchased in quantity and/or special sales by contacting the author or publisher at:
Resilient Publications
1805 S. Bellaire Street, Suite 175
Denver, CO 80222
margit@margithenderson.com

Cover and Interior Design: Nick Zelinger (NZ Graphics)
Editing: Craig Lancaster (Lancarello Enterprises)
Illustration: Gigi Willett
Action-Able Map Image: Paul Vorreiter

Library of Congress Control Number: 2020922985
ISBN: 978-0-9905189-2-1 (print)
ISBN: 978-0-9905189-3-8 (eBook)

First Edition

Printed in the USA

For Caity and Theo,
my beacons of hope

Contents

Your Road Atlas for Change

In the days before GPS—before your phone could guide you with a live map and talk you through each turn—most of us had a tattered, oversized road atlas stuffed under our car seat. When planning a road trip, we'd look at the map of the U.S. to get the big picture and then flip through the pages of alphabetized state maps to find the relevant one for charting the specific course to our destination. The same atlas could be used to travel from Atlanta to Boston, from Lincoln to Indianapolis and from Houston to Santa Fe.

This book is your road atlas for change—it covers a lot of ground. I summarize the process of change overall, illuminate the most common obstacles disrupting change and guide you to the paths around and through these challenges to keep you on course. To show you how change unfolds, I share examples from my own change journeys and introduce you to fellow travelers whose stories are woven through these pages. Each section has activities to deepen your experience and learning process.

A road atlas shows all the roads, but you travel only the specific highways and streets going to your destination. Similarly, on your change journey, you won't need every concept covered in this book. Your job is to identify the road-block you're facing now and do the exercises relevant to the current part of your journey.

By picking only the relevant exercises, you will customize the path for your unique personality and situation. Just as there are several routes from Denver to Los Angeles, each navigating through or around the mountains and deserts in between, the route that works for you will likely be different from someone else's even if you're pursuing the same goal.

Once you've read the book through and handled your first obstacles, then use it as a reference. You can keep coming back to this atlas to orient yourself for each next segment of your journey until you get to your change destination. Plus, down the road, you will have another change goal. Some of the things you learned on your first change adventure will apply again, but you will also hit other challenges specific to the new issue. It will be time to dust off your change atlas, flip through these pages and map a path to your next new habit. Over time, I hope this book will be tattered, marked up and well used—just like the dog-eared old road atlas that accompanied me, laid open on the passenger seat, helping me find my way.

Do you remember being in charge of your first big road trip? It might have been hard to think through all the logistical details and navigate the roads to your destination. But once you got the hang of taking road trips, it got easier and easier, even when you were venturing off to someplace new. The process of transforming hope into lasting change is similar. The first big change is the most challenging. But once you learn the science-based solutions mapped out in this change atlas, you will discover how to live your best intentions.

Chapter Recap

◆ This book offers a detailed, science-based explanation of how change works and how to overcome common roadblocks to change.

◆ Read it through and do the exercises relevant to the obstacle before you now.

◆ Return to this reference book when you hit another roadblock or commit to a new change goal.

<u>Note:</u> Each chapter includes exercises to help you to experience the concepts discussed. Use your own journal to write your reflections, or download the specific exercise worksheet you want at www.margithenderson.com/hope-to-habit-worksheets. Plus, a full recap of the ideas and exercises in this book are provided in a downloadable workbook at this same weblink. Use these resources to customize your change journey.

The Challenging Path to Change

The first hour of our walking tour in the Costa Rican rainforest is lovely, just as the guidebooks promised. We marvel at the lush tropical plants and try to spot the camouflaged creatures surrounding us. The light filters through the thick canopy and vines upon vines climb every tree. The sounds of birds and howler monkeys fill the air. Venturing across dramatic suspension bridges, we take in the stunning vistas and watch for movement on the forest floor below.

An hour before, ten of us spilled out of our van, eager to stretch our legs after the long morning drive from the coast, north and inland to Arenal's Hanging Bridges. Our extended family gathered in Costa Rica to celebrate my father's 81st birthday.

As we walk through the park, our naturalist guide narrates our surroundings. You can imagine the kids' delight when the guide gathers us around to peer into the hole where the park's host tarantula lives. "Go for it," I offer, stepping back decisively, thinking to myself, "No way!" I'm squeamish about creepy-crawly things so I have no intention of putting my face near the door of the tarantula's hidey-hole.

I probably have my brother to thank for this. When we were kids, he was the classic pesky little brother—I don't remember, but he might've tossed a spider into my hair, relishing my shriek. Now nearly 50 years old, my brother is a professional mountain man. He lives in upstate Montana, owns a mountaineering store and is comfortable and capable in the wild. I, on the other hand, am an uptight city slicker. We grew up in Washington D.C., and then I moved to Chicago before settling in Denver. My laidback brother used to accuse me of being a control freak, and I must confess he's right. A manicured English garden is more my cup of tea than the Costa Rican rainforest. Yet Arenal is dramatically more beautiful than anywhere I've ever been. So here we are, my brother and I, gathered with our families around the tarantula's hole. I slow my breathing, trying to relax.

At this point on the nature tour, my father's right there with us. He's vigorous for his age. He lifts weights, swims regularly and in his late 60s, he completed a triathlon and won first place, because he was the only entrant in his age group. This 1.9-mile nature walk seems manageable to him. But while the experience of the Hanging Bridges Park is described as "walking on air," as though you float from one scenic overlook to the next, what isn't mentioned is the steepness of the paths going down and up sizable hills between the park's fifteen bridges.

We had arrived by mid-afternoon when light could fight its way through the thick foliage. As we come to the early intersection where the "accessible" trail peels off for a shorter walk, my father pauses but decides to stay with the group to explore the full trail. I walk with him up and down the slippery hills. The paths are mostly well maintained, often with handrails, but as we trudge up and down and up and down, he becomes fatigued and begins to slow down. I stay back with him, admiring the flowers and birds. Our group stretches out as the kids excitedly explore ahead.

By now, we're several hours into our hike and my father is really struggling. With nowhere to sit to restore his strength, he's lumbering forward, one exhausted step at a time. Twilight is creeping in and, it seems to me, so are the critters. The animals are getting noisier as dusk descends, and most of the park guests have departed. My skin crawls as I imagine what might drop out of the trees and onto my head.

Suddenly my twelve-year-old nephew stops short and points, "Snake!" I glance ahead in the dim light and see what looks to me like a stick on the path. But when the naturalist shines his flashlight nearby, it moves. My heart lurches. Eyes wide, I hold my breath. The guide uses a green laser light, moving it ahead of the snake in short strokes, pretending to be prey, hoping to coax it off the trail. The snake follows the light and slithers into the underbrush.

My anxiety surges, and I want to run. I cannot get out of there fast enough, but we have another half-mile to go and must stay together. My father is taking one slow step at a time, gripping the handrail. I stay by his side. As our group inches along, I ask the guide what kind of snake it was. "Fer-de-lance," he answers without elaboration. I try to calm myself, remembering how small it was. When I look it up online that evening, my breath quickens again at the description: "The fer-de-lance is considered the most dangerous snake in Costa Rica, irritable and fast moving, a highly venomous pit viper."

Never before have I been so relieved, as we stumble out of the now-dark forest, into the shuttered park entrance and the otherwise empty parking lot. My father has valiantly dragged himself to the finish line after three hours of walking steep hills. We collapse into the safety of our waiting van.

————— • —————

Usually, I get to be the guide, leading people through their uncharted emotional territory using a map I know well. Over the past 30 years, in my work as a clinical psychologist, I've helped hundreds of people on their journeys to lasting change. Together, we've contended with threatening predators, including suicidal depression, trauma, addiction and anxiety. My clients have realized their hopes of becoming better partners, parents, friends and professionals. Using science-based solutions, I've taught them how to build self-care routines, to develop effective communication and conflict skills, to manage and tolerate their emotions and to be more compassionate with themselves and others. My clients have turned around their mental and physical health, saved their marriages and become more productive at work. As a guide, I've oriented folks to the path, helped them avoid pitfalls, encouraged them at each step and celebrated with them as their lives have flourished.

I am also a fellow traveler. Like my father during our Costa Rican trek, I have endured life challenges that left me so weary, I wasn't sure I could take another step. But with encouragement and guidance, I staggered onward and found the way to live my best intentions. These experiences, while grueling, are also my life's most triumphant moments, and I look back and feel proud. I've worked to understand myself, find contentment and become a better spouse, parent, friend and professional. Drawing from what I've learned from my own journey as well as by guiding others, I have spent years developing a new path for you. The workers at Arenal Hanging Bridges Park cleared a trail through the rainforest, laying down paving stones one at a time and building bridges and handrails. Similarly, I have laid out a road for you by examining the research on behavior change and applying these ideas in my clinical work and in my own life.[1] In the upcoming pages, I will share with you the Action-Ability Approach, my step-by-step process for transforming hope into habit.

I have traveled this trail myself countless times. I know the ups and downs, the dangers and the places to hold on. Throughout this book, I will share with you examples from my life when I've used the Action-Ability Approach to create lasting change for my own health, relationships and work.

I haven't found a way to make this experience feel "like floating on air." The hills on the journey to change will be steep at points, and sometimes your footing will seem unsure. You will probably get tired. But I will be by your side for every step. I'll make sure there's plenty of daylight, and I've built benches along the way so you can restore your energy.

I promise the changes you create for yourself will be worth your perseverance on this journey! Your dreams of a healthier, happier, more fulfilling life are possible when you learn how to take charge of your actions.

How do you want your life to change? Maybe you're trying to exercise regularly, manage your finances better or stop procrastinating. You realize you could feel more energetic, financially secure or successful, and you're motivated to change. Or maybe you've received an ultimatum from your boss, your spouse or your doctor that your actions need to change or else. You've heard their feedback that you ought to stop smoking, be more attentive at home or be more effective at work. You're scared to lose your job, your marriage or your life.

You *want* to change. You've probably even tried before. You have the right intention, yet it's challenging to stay on track. You're not alone. Most people make resolutions that go by the wayside within days. Usually, people come back to their good intention again and again but are unable to maintain lasting change. As W.C. Fields joked of his attempts to quit drinking, "It's easy. I've done it a thousand times."[2] Making a different choice a few times might be simple, but how do we really change for good?

Creating lasting change requires you to develop healthy new habits. Living your best intentions is easy once you've done the work to make the action habitual, because then it's self-sustaining. The Action-Ability Approach illuminates the path to changing unwanted habits into new healthy habits.

Habits are at the root of both the struggles and the successes of our lives. Our unhealthy habits cause suffering for us and our loved ones, and our healthy habits set us up for success in work, love and play.

The distinction between healthy and unhealthy habits isn't always as clear as it might seem. For example, exercising regularly might be healthy, but we can exercise excessively to avoid our anxiety and can even create a health risk by pushing ourselves too hard. Being highly productive might be a healthy habit, or we might overwork to avoid the strain in our relationship rather than addressing it. Being off task might be an unhealthy habit, or it can be an act of self-care to rest regularly.

Creating habits is easy because *our brains are habit-formation machines.* When we repeat a behavior over and over, our brain cells communicate with each other and develop cellular pathways that enable the action to happen automatically. The problem is unhealthy habits are easier to create than healthy ones. Our unhealthy actions don't require as much effort to repeat and are often immediately and/or intensely rewarded, motivating us to do them again. By contrast, healthy actions have distant rewards and require effort to repeat, so they are less likely to get the repetitions that form the brain pathways and create a habit.

Habits happen. The question is: Will you choose your habits or will your habits choose you?

I am here to show you how to take charge of your life by *owning* your habits.

——— • ———

Our resolutions for healthy habits are like tadpoles. Frogs, like the ones teeming in the Costa Rican rainforest, lay hundreds of eggs, resulting in countless little tadpoles. But most tadpoles die before becoming baby frogs, and many of these froglets don't make it to adulthood. Predators and lack of nourishment cull the young frogs, and only the few luckiest and strongest survive to adulthood.

Similarly, not every good intention becomes a habit. In fact, very few do. Most ideas for change die in the resolution phase or shortly thereafter. We feel inspired to better ourselves. "I will eat healthier." "I'll be more patient with my children." "I'm going to stop gambling." We make a resolution with sincerity, but within hours or days, our old habits resurface and we give up on our good intention, returning to our usual patterns.

When we learn to carefully consider our resolution tadpoles, select the most important ones and create a supportive habitat, we are much more likely to live our best intentions.

The Stages of Habit Development

The lifespan of a habit has four stages.[3] Stage 1 is the Resolution Phase. Typically, we just grab hold of a change idea and declare our intention to act without giving our resolution any thought. This is a setup for failure. In Part I of this book, I will teach you solutions for choosing and incubating your hopes to protect them from the predators that otherwise pick off your good intentions. By learning how to manage the resolution selection process in Part I, you will ensure your resolution is hearty and strong—fit for action.

Stage 2 is Preparation, where we transition our resolution from a thought to a behavior. Usually, resolutions die from lack of preparation. We declare our intention and spring into action, feeling passionate about the goal. Like a tadpole sprouting legs, our idea is on the move. We resist the shopping spree, the donut or the argument. We get up early to go to the gym or get right to work. But usually this surge of action fizzles out when we get distracted or discouraged. As motivation wanes, old habits kick back in and resolve falters. In Part II of this book, you will learn how to improve your resolution survival rate by devoting your preparation to setting up a nourishing and protective habitat for your new behavior. Part II explores the Preparation Phase for creating lasting change, where you will discover how to prepare your mind, relationships and environment for change.

Stage 3, the Sustained Action Phase, can be the most difficult to get through. If a resolution even makes it this far, it usually dies here. But using the Action-Ability Approach, you've prepared a nourishing ecosystem to strengthen your resolve and you've removed predators to protect your behavior change. You stay with your commitment, repeating your behavior over and over, avoiding resolution predators, including distraction, craving, anxiety, boredom and lapses. Even so, every successful behavior change falters along the way, but now you will succeed because the mindset you developed in the Preparation Phase will enable you to regroup quickly and return to the intention again and again. In Part III, I will teach you resolution first aid so that when your new behavior takes a hit, you will know how to patch it up and return to sustained action.

Once your resolution has fully matured, it's on autopilot in Stage 4, the Habit Phase. You've done countless repetitions of your desired behavior during the Sustained Action Phase, which established new networks in your brain so your behavior happens with less effort and thought. The Habit Phase is the reward we craved when we declared our hopeful intention.

This book is a science-based guide explaining the Action-Ability Approach for how to raise a new behavior from a fledgling resolution to an adult habit. We will explore each developmental stage and identify the pitfalls and predators as well as phase-specific solutions for survival. Once you understand how to protect and nourish your change ideas, you will have a process for transforming your hope into healthy habits.

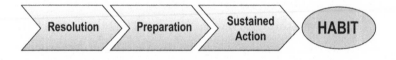

The Action-Ability Approach
Stages of Habit Development

The saying goes: Knowledge is power. But here's the truth: Knowledge is potential—*implementation* is power.[4] By harnessing the Action-Ability Approach, you will turn the potential of your ideas into lasting change. When you transform what you know into action, the power to live your best life is unleashed.

Chapter Recap

- Lasting change requires us to create healthy new habits.

- The brain is a habit-formation machine. Will you choose your habits, or will your habits choose you?

- When we repeat a behavior over and over, our brain cells communicate with each other and develop cellular pathways that enable the action to happen automatically.

- This book describes the Action-Ability Approach, which will empower you to take charge of your life by owning your habits.

- The Action-Ability Approach is a step-by-step process for lasting change, moving through four phases from Resolution through Preparation and Sustained Action to Habit.

Key Words

Action-Ability Approach, Resolution, Preparation, Sustained Action, Habit

PART I:

RESOLUTION PHASE

Promises, Promises

R achel feels sick to her stomach. The rage drains out of her in an instant. Her son is cowering in the corner, curled up and ashamed. Shocked, she can feel the sting on her hand, her pale palm still red from having slapped him. She realizes she's hulking over him.

Rachel steps back. Her hands pull close to her body and then cover her face. Tears flood from the spot now vacated by anger. "Oh, no! No," she sobs. "What have I done?" Drawn to comfort her son, Rachel shifts as if to step toward Jason. He flinches, covering his head.

Recoiling against the opposite wall, Rachel slides to the floor, consumed with remorse. "That can never happen again," Rachel declares to herself. "This time I really mean it."

Regret is a powerful motivator, but it usually leads to unfulfilled promises, not to real change. If, like Rachel, we've hurt someone we love, our anguish can feel overwhelming. But equally distressing is the shame we feel when we can't follow through on commitments we have made to ourselves. We regain the weight we lost. We receive a poor evaluation at work because we can't get organized and regularly miss deadlines. We make another promise to ourselves. This is it. This time, we'll really change.

To make effective resolutions, we need to understand why we make promises in the first place. We think we make resolutions because we want to change our behavior, but usually we make a promise because we want to change *how we're feeling in the moment*. We feel upset, uncomfortable, embarrassed or envious, and the new behavior we're eyeing seems to offer a path to relief. Just the thought of our resolution allows us to exhale and feel a bit better.

An hour later, Jason is in his room, music blaring. Rachel knocks and pokes her head in, wincing. Jason turns to her and can see her soft expression, her green eyes bloodshot from crying. "Can I talk with you?" she asks gently. He shuts off the music.

Rachel's genuine remorse pours out, as she apologizes for hurting him. Jason already knows his mother was physically abused as a kid by her own parents, and he sees she's trying to make different choices with him. Rachel doesn't make excuses—she knows she needs to handle her anger better. But she hasn't figured out how yet. All she has at this point is another promise, though it's wearing thin. Jason has heard it too many times before. Even so, they are both relieved to feel softer and safer with each other, at least for now.

Resolution making can be a habit in and of itself, regardless of whether it leads to real change. We promise ourselves or someone else that we will change because, in the moment, it makes us and them feel better. When Rachel apologizes to Jason, her shame eases and she feels the relief of reconnecting with him. Just the action of declaring our best intention is rewarded like any other habit.

The Habit Pathway

Rewards drive behavior and habit formation. Actions followed by a positive experience or by relief from a negative experience tend to be repeated. Your brain wants to get the reward again, so it pays close attention to spot the feelings, situations and actions happening beforehand so it knows how to re-create the rewarding situation. These details are cues or signs pointing in the direction of the reward.

I don't remember meeting my first potato chip and discovering the rewarding experience of eating it, but I know my tongue's happiness told my brain, "Again, again! Let's figure out how to have that experience again." This kicked my brain into action to identify the signs and pathways to future chip encounters. My brain noted what chips look and smell like (signs that the happy taste is coming) and remembered I need to reach for a chip and put it into my mouth (actions taken to get the reward).

The brain usually analyzes rewarding experiences without your having to consciously think about it. Behind the scenes, your brain is creating a detailed map of the roads back to rewards: Signs (cues) – Travel (actions) – Destination (rewards).[1]

Your brain also generates fuel for the journey. The excited anticipation of the reward energizes you to take action. When I see and smell chips, my mouth waters as I crave the experience of eating them. I want the chips and I'm not eating them yet—this creates a tension I feel compelled to resolve. I want to feel differently. When I pick up the chip and put it in my mouth, my craving is satisfied for the moment and I enjoy the rewarding, crunchy, salty taste sensation. My mouth is watering even now as I write this description. The power of craving is in the mind's capacity to anticipate, to imagine the experience, and this creates desire.

Now your brain has its travel plan: Look for the road Signs (cues) that the reward is ahead, which Fuels you with excitement (craving). This longing motivates you to Travel (take action) to the Destination (reward).[2] My potato-chip-eating habit was created by my traveling this pathway over and over. My brain watches for Signs (seeing and smelling chips), fills me with Fuel (excited anticipation of the chip taste) to motivate me to Travel (get chips and put them into my mouth) to arrive at my Destination (rewarding, crunchy, salty chip experience).

THE HABIT PATHWAY

Now let's apply the understanding of the Habit Pathway to the habit of making resolutions. We want the positive reward our new behavior will bring—the promotion at work, being able to fit into a favorite outfit again, feeling closer with our spouse. *But often what we want even more is relief from the negative experience we're having right now.* I've eaten too many chips and have a bellyache, so I swear off chips. Rachel feels ashamed about hurting Jason. She wants her anguish to stop, so she promises never to hit him again.

When the reward is relief, the brain knows a short road to get there: make a promise to change and whew! We feel better already. No need to Travel the long, steep road to actually making the change itself, because we've gotten the reward of relief from the action of declaring our good intention.

False Hope Syndrome happens when we don't follow through on our resolution because we feel relieved enough by the experience of making a promise that we aren't motivated anymore to do the work to follow through.[3] By making a promise, we reconnect with the person who's mad or disappointed in us, or we reassure ourselves that we won't make that mistake again. The promise shifts our mood from despair to hope, from guilt to absolution, from shame to pride. The action of making resolutions is rewarded. For example, an alcoholic wakes up after a binge to an angry partner and a wicked hangover and responds with a sincere promise to stop drinking. This genuine resolution might be enough to soothe the guilt and restore the relationship. Both partners feel hopeful about this fresh start, and the tension is resolved. But in the days and weeks to come, the work of sobriety (Travel) goes by the wayside because the promise created relief and now there isn't enough motivation (Fuel) to persist toward true change.

A resolution that makes it all the way to a new habit is a true source of accomplishment and pride. But when we break our promises to ourselves and others over and over, our

disappointment, guilt and shame are amplified. Resolutions
that fail feed our distress and leave us feeling badly about ourselves and strain our relationships. We can make ourselves
feel better again, temporarily, by making another promise for
change—"I really mean it this time"—but now we are at risk
of getting tangled in a vicious Shame Loop.

Fail to
Follow
Through

Feel Guilt,
Shame, Regret
(Sign)

Rewarded by
Relief, Hope
(Destination)

Crave Relief
from Distress
(Fuel)

Promise to
Change
(Travel)

The Shame Loop

If you're in the habit of making and breaking promises,
then I invite you to develop a new habit of making only
actionable resolutions, and I will show you how.

A doable resolution will offer you the quick relief from
regret, plus it will spare you from the Shame Loop and put
you on track for genuine pride in yourself. In the meantime,
rather than declaring "I will change," reword this to emphasize
"I want to change" or "I can change."

The word resolution comes from the Latin root word *resolutionem*, which means *to loosen*. If our problem is a convoluted knot, our resolution intends to untangle it. But making a quick, poorly thought out resolution is like yanking on a loose end, inadvertently causing the knot to tighten. When we declare our best intention and fail to follow through, we're in worse shape than we were before. We feel discouraged, ashamed, regretful, defensive or unreliable. Instead, the better plan is to loosen the center of the knot to see how the ball of rope is woven together, to see the cord's path so you can untangle it. By taking the time to understand the problem, we are better positioned to resolve it and can harness *true hope* for lasting change.

"I'll make the marketing calls I've been avoiding." "I will manage my stress better." "I'll go for a walk daily." What promises do you make to yourself and others?

My current promise to myself and my family is *I will stop micromanaging my adult children*. All forms of my reminding, suggesting, coaxing, nagging or otherwise trying to direct them are included. I should have done this a long time ago, but I've already confessed to you that I'm a control freak, so you're probably not surprised this is a struggle for me. My kids are now home from college for the summer, so we're going to drive each other nuts if I don't work on this. Both of them are thoughtful, responsible and kind young people. Really, my work here is done. I need to give them space to make their own choices and mind my own business. But my bossiness is a convoluted knot. I've tried before to stop this long-standing, ingrained habit, and like the boy who cried wolf,

I'm at risk of losing my credibility. This will be my resolution while I keep you company on your journey for change. Let's do this together. My kids will thank you!

To stop making empty promises, effective resolutions focus on the *lasting rewards* of our new habit. When we stick with our best intentions for change, how will it make our lives better? Something important is motivating you to read this book and do the work to create your new habit. What outcome are you seeking? What sparks your hope?

Our reasons for wanting to change are unique and personal. Two people with the same resolution may well be motivated by different outcomes. Maybe I focus on saving money to pay down debt while you save for a trip. You might work on eating healthier to bring down your cholesterol while I strive to change my eating because I want to lose weight. I might want to improve my listening skills to be a better parent whereas you're motivated to listen carefully at work to become a more impactful manager. We can have the same resolution yet be motivated by different outcomes.

What's your core motivation for working on the new habit you've selected? For starters, just claim the first reason that comes to mind for why your new habit matters to you. We will come back to this issue again and again, elaborating our reward experience to keep us Fueled for Travel through the Sustained Action Phase.

The lasting benefits of our potential resolution offer us a north star to guide our journey. We keep the star in mind even when it's hidden by clouds. The star might be far away, but orienting to it keeps us pointed in the right direction. I want to stop micromanaging my children because my bossiness undermines them in discovering their own confidence and strains their connection with me. Rachel is motivated to stop raging at Jason because she wants to break the cycle of abuse and have a closer relationship with her son than she has with her parents. Keeping these important outcomes in mind helps us find a path to real change.

Action-Able Exercise R1:
Pick your first potential resolution

What behavior do you want to change? Feel free to pick something easy, such as pausing every hour at work to stretch. Or you might have an urgent and challenging goal. Maybe you've had a health emergency and the doctor has given you strict orders to exercise vigorously three times per week.

Be sure the behavior you pick is your own. If you're focused on changing someone else's behavior, such as the actions of an employee, child or spouse, consider what part of the dynamic is your responsibility. Think about how you can improve your management, parenting or relational style to bring out the best in this person. Even if your goal is to be a catalyst for someone else's improvement, the target always needs to be your behavior.

Pick ONE potential resolution to work with for our exploration of the Resolution Phase. Avoid making a grand declaration. For now, instead of wording it as a resolution "I will . . ." for starters, state it is a possibility: "I can . . ."

Write your potential resolution:

I can _____

_____.

Next, what reward are you seeking with your potential resolution?

I want to _____,

because _____.

Chapter Recap

◆ We often make promises because we want to change the regret or shame we're feeling in the moment. To make a resolution we will really follow through on, we need to orient to powerful and lasting motivations (rewards) for change.

◆ A habit is developed because the behavior is rewarded. The brain figures out how to experience the reward again and creates a Travel plan looking for Signs (cues) that the reward is ahead, which Fuels you with excitement (craving). This longing motivates you to Travel (take action) to the Destination (reward).

◆ False Hope Syndrome happens when we don't follow through on our resolution because we are rewarded enough with relief by the action of making a promise so we aren't motivated anymore to do the work to follow through.

◆ A Shame Loop happens when we make and break promises over and over, each time declaring "this time I really mean it."

◆ Rather than declaring "I will change," for now focus on "I can change" or "I want to change, because. . ."

◆ Focus on the lasting rewards of your new behavior to stay motivated for the work of building your new habit.

Key Words

Habit Pathway, Sign, Fuel, Travel, Destination

Clarify Your Resolution Challenge

Jasmin cups her hands in her lap, wishing she could hide her gnawed off fingernails. She tries to pay attention to the interviewer's question and come up with a compelling answer, but she's flooded with self-consciousness. She chewed her nails non-stop this past week—her nervousness about this job interview was overwhelming. She really wants this graphic design job, but it's probably a long shot. Her hands seem to reveal her stress.

"Ms. Patel?" The interviewer's prompt snaps Jasmin's attention back to the discussion. She searches her mind. *What was the question?*

Jasmin hates that she can't stop biting her nails. It's such a stupid little habit, she thinks, but it leaves her feeling distracted, vulnerable and exposed.

Even minor habits, like Jasmin's nail-biting, can leave us feeling out of control when we struggle to change a seemingly simple behavior. Sometimes small resolutions are the most challenging to get a handle on because they start outside of our awareness. You slouch without realizing it even though you want to convey confident body language. Or you bark at your assistant before you can catch your terse words. Like countless little cuts, these quick actions can add up and do major harm. What they all have in common is they begin absent-mindedly.

The behaviors we resolve to change can be grouped into three general categories: absent-minded, obsessive or avoidant.[1] The problems in the Habit Pathway are different for each of these three dynamics. By learning to read the map of the Habit Pathway for our resolution, we can orient to the best change approach for our unique situation.

Jasmin wants to stop the absent-minded behavior of biting her nails, but her fingers are in her mouth before she realizes what she's doing. Behaviors with an absent-minded dynamic have Sign problems. We don't notice the Signs of the absent-minded behaviors we want to stop, or there aren't any Signs for the behaviors we want to start. We intend to floss our teeth regularly but don't remember to do so. We mean to take the new medication our doctor prescribed, but we keep forgetting. When we figure out the right Signs, the new action is easy to take. The key to a resolution with an absent-minded dynamic is to discover the subtle Signs of a behavior we want to stop or put up Signs for a behavior we want to start.

Reflecting on my micromanaging, I realize sometimes suggestions pop out of my mouth absent-mindedly. This ingrained habit probably began as soon as I could form sentences—I was the classic bossy big sister. When my mother's long-term illness hit, my grasping for control amped up. At age 10, I became a little mama, trying to hold our family together. Add to that twenty years of parenting my own children, where directing is sometimes necessary and appropriate, and I have almost 50 years of bossiness under my belt! Now it happens so automatically that sometimes I issue commands without even seeing them coming. But other times, I'm overwhelmed with parental worries that Fuel an obsessive version of my micromanaging.

Behaviors with an obsessive dynamic are driven by consuming thoughts and emotions pushing toward an unhealthy habit, which creates a seemingly uncontrollable urge to act. There is nothing absent-minded about these experiences—instead, the mind is preoccupied with the burning desire to take action. When a resolution targets an obsessive dynamic, there's a Fuel problem. The craving is overwhelming. These are generally behaviors we want to stop.

When Rachel is filled with rage, she's consumed by the urge to lash out. She sees Jason's muddy footprints tracked across the beige carpet and her body roils with anger. Rachel's memories of being abused as a child disappear as her wrath surges. She feels justified, ready to condemn Jason. Rachel is grappling with an obsessive dynamic.

When my micromanaging becomes obsessive, it's Fueled by fear. During my childhood, I reacted to anxiety about my mom's life-threatening illness by trying to control my environment and the people around me. As an adult, I have the usual parental worries plus some legitimate additional concerns given the unique challenges my kids face. But I can amplify these worries into harrowing catastrophes that seem to require my immediate intervention. I realize I shouldn't meddle and try to restrain myself, but my anxiety drives me forward as I devise sneaky ways to "have a conversation" about the threatening scenario I imagine I need to avert. When my nagging is obsessive, my mind spirals with worries and my body is agitated by fear. Like Rachel, my emotion pushes me toward actions that harm my relationships with my children.

The same action, such as nagging or eating a pint of ice cream, could be done absent-mindedly or obsessively. If I've spent the whole drive home fantasizing about the ice cream, the urge getting stronger and stronger, the craving overpowering the healthy intention, then I have an obsessive dynamic to deal with. If, on the other hand, I grab the ice cream container while preoccupied with the troubles of my day, flop on the couch, spoon in hand, digging in while focused on the TV, then this behavior has an absent-minded dynamic. Once I notice, I can stop. By learning to read the map of the Habit Pathway, you can design a more effective resolution and prepare better for sustained action.

In some cases, a behavior with an obsessive dynamic starts absent-mindedly. You might reach for your cigarettes habitually, lighting up without awareness. To clarify whether this action has an absent-minded or obsessive dynamic, notice what happens next. If you catch yourself and can easily put out the cigarette, reminding yourself of the resolution to cut back, then this is an absent-minded dynamic. But if your craving surges when you notice yourself smoking and you feel like you can't put out the cigarette without finishing it, then you're dealing with an obsessive dynamic.

Different yet again, resolutions with an avoidant dynamic have problems with the Travel and Destination. Our hope points us to a healthy behavior we value, but we end up on a detour instead. We know we should eat more veggies, but we keep ordering the french fries. We ought to do the difficult task at work, but we binge watch our favorite show instead. We need to have the hard conversation with our partner, but we're scared to bring it up.

When we grapple with an avoidant dynamic, we're at a crossroads. The Travel to live our best intention is longer and more challenging to navigate. We want the reward (Destination) of eating healthier, accomplishing the task at work or communicating with our partner, but the path to get there feels too difficult. So we take a detour to Travel on an easier road. The Destination of the easy path is relief. When we avoid the hard decision, task or conversation, we're rewarded by lowered stress. But our avoidance also creates disappointment when our health, work and relationships continue to suffer.

Again, note that the same behavior could have an obsessive dynamic or an avoidant one. For example, for some people online shopping is just used as a distraction, while others shop compulsively. The main distinction is the experience of Fuel. The urgency Fueling an obsessive action is so overpowering that we blow right through the crossroads, barreling toward the unhealthy action without even noticing the turn for the road to our resolution. In contrast, the experience of an avoidant dynamic feels like we're running out of Fuel.

There's not enough gas in the tank to get up the hill to our resolution. We pause at the crossroads, torn, before turning to coast downhill. The experience of an obsessive action is that we feel propelled *toward* something enticing, while the experience of an avoidant dynamic is of moving *away* from something unpleasant or stressful. The thought of the action we're supposed to do makes us feel anxious, annoyed or apathetic, so we turn away from it and take a detour.

I was a devoted couch potato for the first 40 years of my life. Sedentary was my preferred state, but when I hit my own midlife health crisis, I realized I needed to get moving. I remember vividly the moment my manual therapist commented, "Your chi is stagnant." I had no idea what this meant, but it sounded bad and it felt true. I imagined my depleted life energy pooling in my ankles, far from my weary heart and mind. I knew I ought to work out, but I dreaded doing it. I told myself I didn't have time, but as my life shifted and more time became available, I acknowledged the truth: I just didn't want to exercise. Sweating felt gross to me, and working out was mind-numbingly boring. I was avoiding exercise, but my health needed me to stop seeking out detours and commit to working out regularly.

By understanding the unique challenges involved in resolutions of each dynamic type, we discover how best to customize our actions in the Preparation Phase to effectively change our Habit Pathway. For resolutions targeting an absent-minded dynamic, we need to discover the Signs, becoming aware of the subtle cues for an unwanted absent-minded action, or posting lots of Signs to remind us of a new simple action we want to start but keep forgetting. For resolutions addressing an obsessive dynamic, we manage the Fuel problem by learning to cope with strong cravings and pointing our Signs in a new direction. Resolutions for behaviors with an avoidant dynamic require us to recognize the cross-roads and skip the detour. By making the Travel to the healthy Destination easier, we are more likely to choose the path to our best intentions.

Next, consider the intensity level of your resolution challenge. Some behaviors cross over a clinical line where they become more difficult to change. For example, Attention Deficit Hyperactivity Disorder involves an extreme absent-minded dynamic. Addictions and eating disorders have complex obsessive dynamics. Depression, anxiety and trauma have avoidant dynamics. Resolutions for a high-intensity issue will likely require a multifaceted intervention and lots of support.

The Action-Ability Approach is helpful for all levels of intensity. The core Habit Pathway is the same for Rachel as it is for Jasmin, but the hills are steeper when, like Rachel, you're wrestling with more intense suffering. Breaking the hold of severe distress is hard, but doing so is possible and life changing.

You need only to take one step at a time. First, identify the challenge dynamic of your resolution.

Action-Able Exercise R2:
Explore your resolution challenge

Consider the potential resolution you identified in Exercise R1 in terms of the Habit Pathway to clarify the dynamic of your challenge. Which dynamic does your potential resolution target?

Circle your answers:

- My potential resolution involves an absent-minded, obsessive and/or avoidant dynamic.

- The intensity of my resolution challenge is mild, moderate or intense.

Chapter Recap

◆ The dynamics of the behaviors we try to change can be grouped into three general categories: absent-minded, obsessive or avoidant.

◆ Resolutions with an absent-minded challenge dynamic involve problems with the Signs in the Habit Pathway. The absent-minded action you want to stop has subtle cues you aren't paying attention to. Simple actions you want to start but keep forgetting don't have clear Signs to remind you to do them.

◆ If you're consumed by a seemingly irresistible urge to do an action you want to stop, then it has an obsessive dynamic. Obsessive behaviors have too much Fuel. To live our best intentions, we need to learn to cope with cravings (de-Fuel) and create Signs to redirect us.

◆ Goals with an avoidant dynamic involve us taking a detour away from our best intentions. At the crossroads, we pick the easier Travel to the Destination of relief from stress but ultimately end up disappointed. We need clear Signs to orient to our true Destination, make the Travel easier and find ways to re-Fuel to give us enough energy to take the longer road.

◆ By recognizing the intensity of our challenge, we can better prepare for our journey.

◆ By understanding the dynamics of our specific resolution challenge, we can map an Action-Able path from hope to habit.

Key Words

Absent-Minded, Obsessive, Avoidant

Don't Don't

Notice what occurs in your mind when you read the following sentence: *Don't think of a warm chocolate chip cookie, with its chocolate melting as you break the cookie in half to take a delicious bite.*

How'd that go for you? Even with the instruction *not* to imagine it, you probably imagined the cookie anyway. When words come across your mind, the brain can't help but create a picture to go with them.

This is a serious problem when you're trying to resist an obsessive behavior. When you tell yourself "don't smoke a cigarette," your brain immediately conjures up an image of a cigarette. You might see the red circle-slash "no smoking" Sign around it, but you're still thinking of a cigarette. Similarly, when you say to yourself "don't go to the casino," you'll likely imagine a bustling casino, even if you've never set foot in one.

The saying goes: What we resist persists. When we tell ourselves not to do something, our attention lasers in on the forbidden activity, envisioning every enticing detail. Telling yourself "don't" isn't enough. You cannot move toward an absence of something. "Don't get mad" doesn't tell Rachel how to handle her anger better. Even for an absent-minded habit "don't bite your nails" isn't useful to Jasmin.

Figure out a substitute behavior you will do instead. If your target behavior is currently framed in the negative, such as "don't eat junk food," "I will stop lying" or "stop procrastinating," your next step is to reframe your goal in positive terms, for example, "I will eat healthy snacks," "I will tell the truth" or "I will work on this task for at least 10 minutes." For absent-minded habits, the alternative is about paying attention. "I will set an alarm for each hour and check my posture, straightening up when I realize I'm slouching."

Create a detailed plan and visualize what you *will* do during the time when you'd normally do the old habit. Jasmin can rub her fingers when she notices the subtle itch activating her nail-biting. For Rachel, rather than "I want to stop yelling at Jason," the intention can be reframed to "I will be more patient with Jason." Or even better yet, remembering to read the Signs: "I will pay attention to my stress level and learn strategies to calm myself when I feel agitated." Once she's found ways to soothe herself, being patient will be easier.

This is the Action-Ability Approach rather than a resist-ability model. To block an unwanted habit, redirect yourself toward the new action. Now your visualizing mind has something constructive to picture and work toward. Habit expert Jeremy Dean noted that "successfully breaking a habit is much more likely when you have a shiny new, well-planned habit to focus on rather than just thinking about suppressing the old habit."[1]

People grappling with addiction have longstanding and intense urges that are difficult to redirect. Just saying "don't drink" or "don't use drugs" is useless. The 12-step programs for addictions, such as Alcoholics Anonymous, are powerful because they offer many substitute actions. Program participants learn to develop a list of alternatives to drinking or using drugs. Instead, they might call their sponsor for support, go to an AA meeting, pray, take a walk, call a friend or do an act of service for someone else. These options offer new ways to cope with cravings by creating other sources of connection and emotional comfort.

As you learn about what triggers your unwanted behavior, translate your resistance goal into an action plan. If the wording of your resolution includes "don't," "I won't" or "stop," reword it in positive terms: "I will." This way you're always moving toward a new plan instead of blocking an unwanted action.

Another reason to dodge "don't" is the What-the-Hell Effect.[2] Scolding yourself that you can't or shouldn't do something sets it up as a rule, which triggers feelings of defiance. Rules beg to be broken. When you break the rule you set for yourself, it's easier to say "what the hell" and double down on the unwanted behavior. A resistance focus can set you up to indulge—even more than you would have had you not tried to change your behavior in the first place.

A similar defiance gets stirred up by *should* or *ought to* language. When you scold yourself and say, "I should order the salad instead of the fries," your reaction might be "I don't want to and you can't make me." Reword your goal using the *I can* language from Action-Able Exercise R1: "I can order a salad." Or remind yourself of the important lasting reward: "I want to order the salad so I can fit into my favorite jeans again."

As we find stronger motivation to act in our desired direction, we become ready to make an effective resolution. We have identified the new action we will do instead of the action we want to stop and have stated our plan in inviting language. Now it's safer to declare our intention in *I will* terms.

Action-Able Exercise R3:
Translate *don't* or *should* into *I will*

Consider the translation examples below and reword your potential resolution in affirming terms in the space below.

Translate *Don't*	into *I will*
Don't eat junk food.	I will keep nuts in my desk drawer so I eat a healthy snack when hungry.
Don't check Facebook at work.	I will get up to stretch and move when I need a break at work.
I should be a better listener.	I will check in with each of my children at bedtime, listening to the stories of their day.
Don't criticize my employees.	I will offer gratitude to each member of my team daily.
I ought to floss my teeth.	I will post a reminder on my bathroom mirror so I remember to floss each evening.

Write your resolution in positive terms:

I will _____.

Chapter Recap

♦ A resistance focus can set you up to indulge even
more than you would have had you not tried to
change your behavior in the first place, because it
can activate the What-the-Hell Effect.

♦ Create a detailed plan for a substitute behavior you
will do instead when you would normally do the
old habit.

♦ If the wording of your resolution includes "don't,"
"I won't" or "stop," reword your resolution in positive
terms: "I will." This way you're always moving toward
a new plan instead of blocking an unwanted action.

♦ Replace "I should" or "I ought to" language with
"I will," "I can" or "I want to, because."

Key Words

I will; I can; I want to, because

Micro-Resolutions

Marcus doesn't understand what his wife wants from him. Kanesha keeps saying he's not listening to her. But he is listening. Marcus is a quiet man, and his wife is a talker. She goes on and on—he does nothing but listen. He hears all the details about Kanesha's sister's new baby. And about how exasperated Kanesha is with Atlanta's horrible traffic. Marcus knows her new boss at the bank is stressing her out. He's listening.

But Kanesha feels disconnected from Marcus and is threatening to drag him to the preacher at their church for marriage counseling. "No way," thinks Marcus, "I can hardly talk to my wife. I sure don't wanna talk to a stranger." When he digs his heels in, Kanesha finds a relationship book for him to read instead. If it gets him off the hook for counseling, he'll read the darned thing.

Marcus scans the table of contents, finds a chapter on listening and flips to that page. Within a few pages, he discovers a secret he didn't know before. Listening to his wife isn't enough. Somehow, he needs to show her that he's heard her. Marcus tends to look down when Kanesha's words are flooding his ears. He hears what she's saying, but he seems tuned out. And maybe, sometimes, he does tune her out.

The book offers a few fairly simple options he's willing to try. The next time Kanesha's talking to him, Marcus looks at her and nods a bit while she's talking. This makes him nervous because it feels like she expects him to say something helpful, and he doesn't know what to tell her. But the book suggests just rephrasing what she's saying to let her know he's heard her. This "reflective listening" idea seems simple enough. While she talks about her frustrations planning her Spelman College 25-year class reunion, Marcus comes up with a sentence and feeds it back to her when she pauses. Kanesha smiles at him.

Last chapter, we explored how small, unhealthy habits, like nail-biting, can leave us feeling out of control, but the good news is small, healthy actions can help us get traction for change.

The saying goes: Every journey begins with a single step. With resolutions, we often want to leap forward, seeking the emotional satisfaction of a big change. However, this approach usually doesn't last. Effective resolutions require fairly easy steps to be taken again and again over a long period, establishing the habit through sustained action.

Micro-resolutions offer a process of taking very small steps over and over and over. While you can have a lofty goal, you cannot get there with one big push.

I am reminded of this truth with each word I type during the l-o-n-g process of writing this book. What you're reading now is the culmination of countless small actions I've taken over the past decades where I have learned, applied and struggled with the concepts I'm sharing with you. I've stepped away and then come back to this project again and again—reading, thinking, talking through, writing and rewriting the ideas you find here. Nothing like writing a book about perseverance to remind me to stick with this project, step by step. Years of small actions led to this moment, as my fingers type away on the keyboard, sustaining my momentum for this otherwise overwhelming project.

A micro-resolution is a commitment to an action taking less than two minutes. As with Marcus, it can be as simple as looking up, nodding and coming up with a sentence rephrasing what his wife just said. He doesn't have to share his innermost thoughts and feelings; he just needs to show her he's paying attention.

My writing goal is often the same as Marcus's: just find a sentence, even if it's awkward. The saying goes: There's no such thing as good writing, only good rewriting. That frees me to write something—anything—just to keep myself moving forward on this project. I know I'll rework each sentence later. Sometimes I hear Dory, the enthusiastic fish from the movie *Finding Nemo*, singing to me, "Just keep swimming," or in my case, "Just keep writing. Just keep writing." Her perky voice helps me persist, one sentence at a time.

Your two-minute resolution can be a goal-related action, like writing the next sentence, or it can be a preparation step that makes your goal more accessible. For example, my habit of regular exercise started with a planning micro-action. One of my friends mentioned she had joined a nearby gym. Inspired, I asked if she would be up for working out together if I joined the gym, too. She was happy to have the company, and we pulled out our calendars to find times that fit for both of our work and parenting schedules. This scheduling micro-action took us less than two minutes and established the timing for our habit of working out together three times per week for eight years now. Blocking out the specific times for exercise and committing to do it together was just what I needed to transform my hope into a workout routine I could stick with. My friend's enjoyable company made me willing to skip the avoidant detour and Travel to my new habit of regularly working out.

Another way to create an exercise habit is to build a series of two-minute actions. It would take less than two minutes to lay workout clothes out each evening so they'll be staring at you in the morning. Once the clothes are there, it takes less than two minutes to put them on the next morning, so this becomes your second micro-resolution. Then, for your third micro-resolution, you can set a two-minute timer on your watch and walk or jog up and down the stairs at your home or apartment. Each of these micro-resolutions is easy to follow-through on, they build on each other and get you into a simple habit of daily exercise. Doing just these three two-minute steps over and over for several weeks, never exercising more than two minutes at a time, begins to establish your pattern of being someone who exercises daily.

A goal of exercising for 30 minutes or more per day requires many other steps. Just finding the time to do a longer workout, not to mention the willingness, confidence, energy, interest, etc., will be challenging. In Part II of this book, you will prepare a path forward for all of those issues. But in the meantime, while you work those details out, daily action on these three two-minute activities (laying out clothes, putting exercise clothes on and two minutes on the stairs) begins to build the habit and identity of someone who works out daily.

Micro-resolutions are easy to follow through on. These steps in the direction of your goal action prepare the path for success. Here are some other examples of two-minute actions that start the process of setting your new behavior up for success.

Goal	Two-minute micro-resolution
I will spend no more than $40 at the mall.	I will remove my credit cards from my wallet and put in $40 in cash.
I will keep nuts in my desk drawer for a healthy snack.	I will write nuts down on my shopping list.
I will get up to stretch and move when I need a break at work.	I will set a repetitive 45-minute alarm on my watch to prompt me to take a movement break.
I will chew gum when I have the urge to smoke.	I will put a pack of gum in the place where I usually keep my cigarettes.
I will thank each member of my team daily.	I will think of and write down a gratitude about one member of my team.

Each of these easy micro-resolutions clears the path for successful future action. Later, when you habitually reach for your cigarettes, you will find gum in your hands and it will be easier to make a healthier choice. At the mall, with your $40 in cash, you can still borrow money from the friend you're with to make the bigger purchase. But rather than a quick credit card swipe, which is easy to do without thinking, getting the extra money will require a conversation with your friend, which will slow down your purchase and give you time to think it through.

Each micro-resolution example is focused on a preparation step for the new action. To eat nuts rather than junk food at work, I must have nuts handy. If I'm going to skip Facebook and do a movement break instead, an alarm will remind me of my intention before my hand makes the habitual click on Facebook.

What kinds of micro-resolutions might fit for your goal? Think about your situation and what will prepare you to do your preferred action. Do you have the supplies you need? Are the things you need in the right locations? Do you have the information you need? Brainstorm about two-minute actions for your first micro-resolution.

Part II of this book explores the Preparation Phase: how to set up the mental, social and physical environment to make Travel easier during the Sustained Action Phase. You will develop many more ideas for micro-resolutions as you continue reading, so for now, just noodle on the kinds of micro-actions that would move you toward your goal.

Developing Awareness

As you have seen, there are no one-size-fits-all solutions to create lasting change. However, awareness is universally required for all change, regardless of the challenge dynamic you face. We need focused attention to discover the unconscious tension driving an absent-minded action, to reduce the Fuel of an obsessive behavior and to prepare compelling cues and rewards help us turn toward our goal rather than an avoidant detour.

My proposal for your first micro-resolution is a two-minute activity that will awaken your awareness. It will also calm your nervous system, clear your thinking, restore your willpower and empower you to take constructive action.

"What two-minute behavior could possibly have such power?" you ask. Drumroll, please—*noticing and slowing your breathing.*[1] Tada!

The micro-action is to set a timer for two minutes and bring your attention back to your breathing over and over until the timer goes off. It's fine to let your mind wander or do something else while you think about breathing. But the main task is to return your attention to the breath and lengthen your exhalations.

As your breathing slows, your body and mind calm down.*
With an exhalation, you can create a conscious pause of your

---

* Slow breathing increases your heart rate variability (HRV). Increased HRV is the biological signature of the Pause and Plan Response, which is the opposite of the physiologically reactive Fight, Flight or Freeze Response. A slow exhalation activates the parasympathetic nervous system, which is the body's calming system.

inner experience, which enables you to make an intentional choice about your action. When stressed, the body amps up, getting ready to fight, flee or freeze, but when we extend our breathing, we create the opportunity for the Pause and Plan Response.[2] By slowing your breath, you take charge of your body's reactivity so you can pause and plan your next action.

Pay attention to your exhalation more so than to your inhalation. Usually a relaxing breath is described as "inhale deeply, then exhale." But if we don't exhale all the way out first, our lungs remain mostly extended and filled with air already, allowing no room for new air to come in. When we're anxious, our breathing becomes shallow, and sometimes we even feel like we can't breathe. Use the muscles between your lungs and your ribcage to squeeze your lungs and push the air all the way out. Then the inhalation will happen with ease.

Slowing your breathing for two minutes seems like a simple instruction, but it will likely be harder than you imagine. "Really?" you might wonder. "I'm breathing all day long anyway. How hard can this be?" The only change during these two minutes is to pay attention to lengthening your exhalation, but it's common to notice one or two breaths and then have your mind get lost in distractions. When your alarm goes off, you might realize you completely forgot to pay attention. This is natural because it's such an absent-minded task. It's boring to think about breathing, and your mind has lots of other thoughts it would rather focus on.

The goal here is not to perfectly attend to two minutes of long exhalations; instead, it's to keep coming back to this micro-resolution and follow through on doing it daily. You get to check the box by taking your first conscious breath. Whatever happens from there is fine. By doing this over and over each day, eventually you'll get better at returning your awareness to breathing more often before the timer goes off.

Another challenge of this seemingly simple task is to remember to do it. Consider pairing your daily conscious breathing exercise with other naturally occurring events that can act as a cue. This two-minute action can be inserted into lots of places during your day: while lying in bed after your morning alarm goes off, when waiting for your coffee to brew or tea pot to whistle, while sitting at a stoplight or in a waiting room, when waiting for the microwave to cook your food, while your car is warming up in the winter, when you turn off your light to go to sleep and *especially anytime you think of your resolution*—notice and extend your breath for two minutes.

In the film *The Karate Kid*, Mr. Miyagi teaches Daniel the fundamental motions of the martial art by training the movements into his body memory using cryptic, repetitive tasks: "wax on," "wax off." While the breathing micro-resolution might seem similarly obscure and unrelated to your goal, it trains your body and mind to activate conscious awareness, which is the first step of every type of behavior change.

Rachel's breakthrough to managing her anger began with learning to slow her breathing. After a month of doing long exhalations for at least two minutes every day, she discovered the subtle differences in her body and mind between when she was calm and when she was agitated. Now she's better able to spot the early signs of becoming annoyed and can slow her breathing, nipping her anger long before it has a chance to ramp up.

Jasmin did her two-minute breathing exercise alternating her focus between her breathing and her fingers. Just to be safe, she tucked her hands under her legs so she wouldn't space out and move them to her mouth. Doing this micro-action enabled Jasmin to recognize the subtle prickling sensations in her fingertips triggering the craving to bite her nails. She also became aware of the tight anxious feeling in her chest Fueling her nail-biting. Now she knows how to calm her nervousness, using slow breathing. And, instead of gnawing on her nails to stop the prickling, she rubs her fingertips on her jeans to calm the tingling. Jasmin's nails are growing, and she's starting to think about the colors of nail polish she will use.

Listening to Kanesha, Marcus also slows his breathing. He feels distracted by the warmth and beauty of her chestnut-colored eyes. He exhales, holding her gaze, and concentrates on crafting his reflection sentence. Now Kanesha can tell he's listening to her. She feels connected and comforted by his calm and steady presence.

You, too, will be more likely to follow through on your best intentions when you have mastered the practice of watching your breath and slowing your exhalation. In our upcoming discussion of the Preparation Phase, we will explore how planning ahead sets up our desired action for success. But for now, remember, the first step toward implementing your resolution is always to pause and exhale so you can be aware and make a new choice.

Action-Able Exercise R4:
Two minutes daily of attention to slow breathing

Your first mission, should you choose to accept it, is to spend at least two minutes each day being aware of your breathing and slowing your exhalations.

Let yourself notice whatever else is going on and just return your awareness to your breathing over and over when you get distracted. Each time you remember to watch your breathing, extend your exhalation. This calms your body and focuses your mind.

Declare your first micro-resolution: For two minutes each day, I will bring my awareness back as often as I can to extending my exhalation.

- What strategies will you use to remember to do this simple task?

- How will you track the timing? Do you have a timer? Or what task will you pair this action with that takes around two minutes?

- How will you keep track of whether you did this task each day?

- Take notes on what helped you succeed with this task and what made it difficult to do.

Chapter Recap

◆ Micro-resolutions set up very small steps that are easy to do and take less than two minutes to complete.

◆ Your two-minute resolutions can be a goal-related action or a preparation step that makes your goal more accessible, like getting supplies, gathering your words, setting reminders or finding information.

◆ Awareness is universally required for all behavior change regardless of the challenge dynamic of your goal.

◆ Consider spending two minutes daily noticing and slowing your breathing, with a focus on exhaling. Acting on this micro-resolution develops awareness, calms the body, clears your thinking, restores willpower and empowers you to take constructive action.

◆ You will be more likely to follow through on your best intentions when you pause, breathe slowly and pay attention to your resolution.

Key Words

Micro-Resolution, Awareness, Exhale

RESOLUTION PHASE
Action-Able Options

▶ Consider your resolutions carefully to prevent the Shame Loop of unfulfilled promises.

▶ Consider the Habit Pathway of the behavior you have resolved to change. Discover the Signs (cues) that Fuel (urge) your Travel (action) to your Destination (reward).

▶ Clarify your resolution by seeing the underlying challenge dynamic: absent-minded, obsessive or avoidant.

▶ Focus on the powerful, healthy and lasting rewards (Destinations) of your goal action, beyond relief from your current distress, to Fuel your Travel to your resolution.

▶ Create a detailed plan for a substitute, healthy behavior you will do instead when you would normally do the unwanted action. Create clear Signs pointing to your resolution.

▶ Make the healthy Destination enticing so it Fuels your Travel.

▶ Use inviting language—"I can" or "I want to, because"—rather than commands such as "don't," "I should" or "ought to" to eliminate the What-the-Hell Effect.

▶ Identify a micro-resolution, taking two minutes or less, preparing for or starting your new action.

▶ Develop your awareness by slowing your breathing, especially when you think of your change goal.

Are any of these Action-Able steps relevant to this moment in your journey? Customize your path using this road atlas to live your best intentions.

Download the relevant exercise worksheets at
www.margithenderson.com/hope-to-habit-worksheets

PART II:

PREPARATION PHASE

Prepare for Success

U sually, we venture forth with our hope calling us like a vacation Destination. It's as if we're inspired by watching the Travel Channel—seeing the gorgeous photos of glistening water, relaxed travelers, delicious food and exciting adventures—and we impulsively charge out of the house, heading to our fantasy. But pretty soon we're standing on the street corner, scratching our head, without luggage, itinerary or travel arrangements. We know where we want to go, but we don't know how to get there.

Countless planning steps are required to get from watching the Travel Channel on your couch to actually arriving at this spectacular beach. You need to find a time in your calendar that will work to be away, arrange to take time off from your job, save enough money to pay for the trip, book the trains, planes and automobiles to get you from your house to your vacation lodging, find your passport, pack your suitcase, etc., etc. Turning hope into habit requires similar preparation. As with traveling, we need to decide where we're going (Resolution), plan the trip (Preparation) and manage the complicated trek (Sustained Action) before we get to enjoy the vacation (the benefits of our habit now that it's easy).

We can visualize our hope, but we need to address the tactical steps of making the dream a reality. You can imagine how great you'll feel with the promotion, weight loss, sobriety or relationship you're pursuing, but you need to work out the path to get there and solve the problems of how to handle the obstacles you'll encounter along the way.

In this section, I will show you how to shape your mental, social and physical environment to make your new action easier. Together, we'll clear the path and prepare you to overcome setbacks so it's easier to persist through the Sustained Action Phase and create your new habit.

Chapter Recap

◆ Rather than just charging toward our resolutions, preparation sets us up for the sustained action that builds our new habit.

◆ This section of the book shows you how to prepare the mental, social and physical environment for success.

Action-Able Mindset

Miranda's face flushes as she feels the waistband of her pants cut into her belly. She feels disgusted with herself for regaining the weight she worked so hard to lose last summer. She hates her body—it's just a fat magnet. No matter what diet she tries, she can't keep the weight off. Last time, Miranda gave away her bigger clothes as a celebration, and she hoped this would prevent her from overeating. Now she feels defeated.

Miranda's not alone. Weight loss is one of the most common and difficult goals people have. While we might be able to manage short-term calorie restrictions, we tend to rebel against deprivation. Our metabolism even slows when we eat less, so keeping weight off can become a battle against our very biology.[1] Most diets set us up for disappointment by offering only an approach for quick weight loss without teaching effective solutions for healthy eating and weight management.

Regardless of what habit you're trying to develop, feeling discouraged—losing hope—is the most common obstacle on the path to behavior change. Even easy micro-actions can be challenging to remember, and as we get to more complex resolutions, setbacks are inevitable.

How we handle our stumbles and frustrations will determine whether we give up or persist on the path to our resolutions. For this reason, developing an Action-Able Mindset is the first step in the Preparation Phase. It's the foundation of all lasting change because it offers a way to transform discouragement into grit for sustained action.

Grit enables us to rally after faltering—to get back up and keep going forward—and it's one of the best predictors of life success.[2] We need to learn how to recommit when we feel discouraged, because creating a new habit requires us to go through a trial-and-error process to find the path that works given our unique circumstances.

Think about the last time you felt disappointed in yourself, discouraged with your attempts to change. Did you spend more money than you planned, give in to the craving for a stiff drink or make a mistake at work? How did you talk with yourself about this setback? Hopefully, you could reassure yourself and recommit to your goal, but it's more common to hear a harsh inner voice that further derails progress. People often call themselves names—lazy, stupid, irresponsible and worse—as they chastise, curse and shame themselves. You might believe you have to be hard on yourself when you lapse, thinking that otherwise you will lose control altogether.[3]

Often, we've learned this harshness from other people's reactions to our struggles. Miranda can still hear the sneering voices of her childhood schoolmates: "Fatty! Morita gordita, you're a slob." Now she piles on herself. Miranda's jaw clenches. "I'm gross." Her chest tightens, and she feels sick with disappointment.

Do you have someone's voice in your head? If you had a harsh parent, teacher or coach, their judgments have likely been internalized. Miranda remembers her Tia Juanita slapping her hand away from the pan of brownies as she reached for seconds. "Mira, that's enough!" Harsh words have staying power and can shape how we react to our own slip-ups.

Action-Able Exercise P1:
Awareness of your current self-talk

How do you talk to yourself when you make a mistake, lose your willpower or forget your intention? Though it can be painful to see in black and white, write down the things you say inside your head when you don't follow through on your resolution and feel disappointed with yourself.

Now imagine saying those words to your dearest friend when s/he is discouraged. It might make you shudder to think of speaking so critically to someone you care about.

Inner harshness is generally intended as a motivational strategy. However, when you scold yourself for slipping on your resolution, you are *less* likely to succeed with your goal.[4] Defensiveness interferes with learning. And worse yet, inner criticism can ignite the internal rebel, activating the What-the-Hell Effect we discussed earlier.

But you don't need to judge your judging. By just observing this scolding *blah blah blah* in your mind, you will be better able to disengage from it. Think about your thinking.[5] Writing down the harsh words you hear in your head lets you see your thoughts and begin to experience this unkind voice as outside of you.[6] Rather than fight with the Inner Critic, just note this judgmental part of you and shift your attention to developing internal support: your Action-Able Mindset.

Compassion

The foundation of the Action-Able Mindset is compassion.[7] Self-forgiveness empowers us to learn about why we got derailed and supports us to get back on track.[8] When we receive our failures with kind accountability, we discover what went wrong and will be more likely to persist after a setback.

Use a compassionate tone when picking yourself up, dusting yourself off and getting back on the path to your resolution. Behavior change is challenging work and inner encouragement, concern and warmth are essential.

If such internal kindness is too much of a stretch for you, work on developing a neutral internal voice. Observe a disappointing experience without editorializing. Just stick with the facts (who, what, when).

For Miranda, developing compassion for herself is difficult. Steeped in our fat-shaming culture, she believes the cruel comments people make so off-handedly about heavy people. For her two-minute slow breathing exercise, Miranda focuses on neutrally inhabiting her body. She notices her chest and belly rise and fall with her breathing. Miranda scans her body from head to toe, observing some basic facts: straight black hair, soft brown skin, hazel eyes. She reminds herself to "keep it neutral," and thinks "curvy body." She exhales and wiggles her toes.

Miranda thinks of her cousin, Yolanda, who also struggles with weight insecurities. Feeling Yolanda's hurt, Miranda feels her chest tighten. She breathes out slowly. Miranda's heart relaxes with the kindness she feels toward Yolanda, enabling Miranda to sit more gently with her own anguish.

Action-Able Exercise P2:
How would you encourage your friend?

Develop compassion for yourself by imagining you're supporting a friend who's hit a setback and feels hopeless. What would you say to encourage your friend to return to the challenge?

Next, write a note or make a voice recording on your phone offering support to yourself for the resolution you're working on. Read or listen to this encouraging message regularly to help you persist.

When you're compassionate with yourself, or at least more neutral, you will be able to pull back and see your situation in a broader context. Remind yourself that setbacks are normal and that your job is to *learn* from what hasn't worked in order to craft a successful approach. Instead of zeroing in on yourself critically, you can look around and figure out what happened.

Inquisitive

The Action-Able Mindset is curious. When you hit an obstacle, be inquisitive rather than judgmental. Adopt a scientist's mind: collect data about what happened to solve the puzzle of why this setback happened.

Your compassionate approach will help you notice things you otherwise would have missed. When you feel discouraged, you will likely turn away from the situation, feeling defeated, defensive or ashamed. The kindness of the Action-Able Mindset is essential because it keeps your eyes open and looking around—it keeps you focused on learning.[9]

A light-bulb moment happens for Miranda when she learns about *Don't Don't*. She realizes her usual diet approaches focus only on what not to eat and set her up to obsess about forbidden food. Don't eat sweets, don't eat carbs, don't eat too much, don't, don't, don't. She moves through the world dodging temptations, feeling deprived and frustrated. Miranda can do this for a few weeks, and she might even lose several pounds, but eventually her resolve cracks. She remembers the last time she broke down and ate two whole cartons of ice cream, at first relieved to buck off the restrictions, but soon curled up with a bellyache, feeling ashamed and disappointed in herself. Miranda winces as she recalls her willpower failing like that, but this time she sidesteps her usual harshness, reminding herself that her experience is shared by so many people, it even has a name: the What-the-Hell Effect. She is not alone. Can she try again using a different approach?

Miranda's next discovery is a game-changer. Through her YouTube feed, she stumbles on CassidyEats. In one video after the next, Cassidy shares about her weight management journey and shows all the delicious-looking and fun food experiments she is trying. Miranda's curiosity stirs. She notices thousands of people have watched Cassidy's videos, too. Miranda reads the comments and sees that others have tried Cassidy's recipes and are losing weight without feeling miserable. There are even recipes for yummy sweets. "Hmm, this might be worth trying," she thinks. Miranda's hope revives. Reading Cassidy's blog posts, watching the videos and trying the recipes give Miranda something to *do*. Cassidy *eats* and this gives Miranda a new way of thinking about her own relationship with food. It's encouraging rather than restrictive and depriving. Now her shopping list has ingredients for Cassidy's latest dessert recipe, so Miranda can bypass the ice cream aisle more easily.

As you can see from Miranda's experience, being inquisitive supports self-discovery. When you're curious rather than critical, you notice details about the situation you overlooked before. Exhaling deeply enables you to pause and plan. These clues will help solve your puzzle so you can revise your plan and recommit to sustained action.

"If there is a secret for greater self-control, the science points to one thing: the power of paying attention," says psychologist Kelly McGonigal, author of the book *The Willpower Instinct*.[10] Your inquisitive mindset strengthens your awareness and orients you to being curious about your resolution and the things that derail or support it.

Be especially curious about your successes. When you make it to the gym as planned, what are the circumstances? When you speak calmly to your child despite your exasperation, how did you do it? What is different when you follow through on your resolution? Understanding the circumstances of your progress is just as important as, and sometimes more so than, learning about your setbacks.[11]

Action-Able Exercise P3:
What sets you up for success?

Think back to the last time you successfully followed through on your resolution. Pick two or three questions from the list below to help you explore *what happened before and after* you stuck with your best intention. This information illuminates the Habit Pathway, showing you the Signs pointing toward your resolution, the Fuel that energizes you to persist and the rewarding Destination of your new action (Travel).

- What was your energy level?
- What was your mood?
- What were you thinking about?
- Was anyone with you? If so, who?
- How connected were you feeling?
- Afterward, how did you feel physically, emotionally and socially?

> • Afterward, what did you think about this experience?
>
> The next time you succeed in following through on your resolution, come back to these questions and deepen your understanding of the circumstances supporting your success.

You are in a discovery process. Like a scientist, watch for patterns in the data you're collecting. What are the circumstances when you succeed? What about when you lapse?

Being inquisitive enables us to see the Habit Pathways of our existing and developing habits more clearly. As Charles Duhigg, author of *The Power of Habit*, points out, "Once you break a habit into its components, you can fiddle with the gears."[12] When you see the cues, cravings and rewards for your actions, you can better understand how to set up future successes and prevent setbacks.

When we get derailed, being compassionate and inquisitive helps us find our way back on track. We discover cues and rewards we missed before. Were you engrossed in your favorite TV show while you finished the whole bag of popcorn when you meant to only eat a few handfuls? Did the blowout sale leave you feeling excited about saving money, distracting you while you overspent your budget? Were you tired when you yelled at your kids?

Be Inquisitive, but remember, this is not an inquisition.

The Inner Critic probably objects to this approach and might even be yelling inside your head right now, "Don't make excuses for yourself. You blew it! I'll whip you into shape so this won't happen again. Forget this compassionate curiosity nonsense." No need to argue with your Inner Critic. Just notice its protests and redirect your thinking back to being a detective, rather than a judge. Just gather up the facts.

Whatever you learn about your situation can be used as an excuse to give up, but your Action-Able Mindset will *transform excuses into problems to be solved*. When we discover a reason we struggle, we've spotted an obstacle to change that needs to be worked out so we stay on course.

You might discover that the Signs point to the wrong Destination. For example, people struggling with addiction are taught to HALT: to look for Signs of being Hungry, Angry, Lonely or Tired, because they are relapse triggers. By catching these known risks for substance use, addicts learn to prevent relapse by resting, having a snack, using a calming strategy or reaching out to a friend.

Observing HALT is a good practice for everyone, because these experiences leave us all feeling vulnerable and weaken our willpower. They certainly put me at greater risk for nagging. Having watched the HALT triggers play out in my life, now I see how the domino effect happens. If I haven't slept well or eaten recently, my depletion leaves me *hangry*. It's not pretty— in fact, I get petty. My grumpiness escalates, and soon I'm lonely, having driven my family away with my nitpicky critical commentary. I grumble and feel sorry for myself, looking to tangle with someone to satisfy my craving for control.

Now I know to HALT instead. If I've had a lousy night's sleep, I make sure to eat well the next day to keep my energy even. I pay extra attention to my mood and slow my breathing to calm my body. If I've had a long, tiring day, I grab a healthy snack before dinner and look for positive ways to connect with my family in the evening. I give my inner control freak the job of addressing these risk factors instead of managing the people around me. By remembering to HALT, I'm much less likely to get grumpy and bossy.

Action-Able Exercise P4:
Reflect on HALT

Consider your own state right now in terms of HALT:

How Hungry are you feeling right now? (circle your answer)

0	1	2	3	4	5	6	7	8	9	10

not at all   somewhat   ravenously
hungry   hungry   hungry

How Angry are you feeling right now? (circle your answer)

0	1	2	3	4	5	6	7	8	9	10

calm   irritable   furious

How Lonely are you feeling right now? (circle your answer)

0	1	2	3	4	5	6	7	8	9	10

connected   somewhat   isolated
                      lonely

How Tired are you feeling right now?
(circle your answer)

0	1	2	3	4	5	6	7	8	9	10
rested				somewhat tired						exhausted

Let any judgment about these observations move across your awareness without latching on to them. Just collect the facts.

Next, think back to a time when you were trying to enact your resolution while you were Hungry, Angry, Lonely or Tired. How did the HALT experiences impact your willpower?

Watch for the need to HALT going forward and collect more observations about the impacts of being Hungry, Angry, Lonely or Tired on your ability to live your best intentions.

You are observing five types of data points: emotions, body sensations, thoughts, social experiences and the physical environment. Developing awareness in these different areas takes some practice. Here are some tips:

- Expand your emotional vocabulary. People often describe themselves as fine, stressed or tired. What emotional words do you use a lot? Strengthen your emotional awareness by digging deeper. What other feeling words can you use to describe your experience? Appendix A offers a list of feeling words to jog your thinking about the nuances of your emotional experience.

- For awareness of body sensations, bring your attention to the top of your head and slowly scan down your body until you reach your toes, noticing where you feel tense and agitated or calm and relaxed. You might practice doing this during your two-minute breathing exercise and watch how your body state changes as your breathing slows. Appendix A also offers language for body sensations to enrich your observations.

- When you watch your thoughts, just pretend you are sitting beside yourself and listen to your mind as if it were a radio. What words are being said? What tone of voice accompanies these words? Awareness of your thoughts is another option you can pair with your daily two minutes of slow breathing.

- Explore your level of social connection. You can feel connected to those you love when you're alone or feel lonely in a crowd.

- Take in the physical conditions around you. Where are you? Is your environment comfortable, stressful or something else? What external cues surround you?

These focal points—emotions, body sensations, thoughts, social experiences and physical environment—will come up again and again throughout the layers of the Action-Ability Approach. There's a lot to be aware of, so don't worry if all of these questions seem a bit overwhelming. Your curiosity will guide you to the most important details, and if you're stuck, try looking at your situation from a new angle using the questions above. There's a path forward. It just might take some extra exploring to find it.

Determined

Determination harnesses your hope and energizes you to live your best intentions. Getting to your goal requires reflective *action*, not reflection alone. The Action-Able Mindset is determined to persist.

Fuel your determination by keeping the rewards for your effort front and center. Remind yourself of the hope you feel about your resolution. Recall what you said in Action-Able Exercise R1: "I want to, because." Plus, what did you discover in Exercise P3 about how you felt after successfully enacting your resolution? What will motivate you to persist? What inspires you to keep trying?

Miranda still wants to lose weight, but she decides to focus on what she will *gain* when she eats. By learning about healthy eating, Miranda discovers how to use food to gain stable energy and positive mood throughout her day. She enjoys eating meals with her family and friends, gaining connection. Inspired by Cassidy, Miranda even finds a playfulness with food, enjoying the colors, smells and flavors as she learns how to cook healthy meals that fulfill her hunger and make her tongue happy.

But Miranda's old relationship with food resurfaces when she's vulnerable. After an exasperating day at work, Miranda finds herself sitting in her car in the grocery store parking lot, finishing the fourth ice cream sandwich out of the box she just bought. She reaches her hand in for the next one and pauses. Miranda exhales, and the tears well up. She realizes her work frustrations trigger her unhealthy eating. She also knows berating herself worsens the pain, making it more likely, not less, that she will finish the box of ice cream sandwiches.

Miranda thinks of her cousin Yolanda and reminds herself to be neutral toward herself, or kind if she can manage it. She thinks back to a blog post she read about regrouping after a food binge. Closing her eyes, she remembers she's not alone. Throwing the box into the backseat, Miranda heads for home. She remembers her goal of using food to *gain* connection, stability and enjoyment in her life. Miranda has also lost 10 pounds in the past two months. Those ice cream sandwiches might set her back a bit, but not if she resets her focus on eating in a healthy way. Her determination and hope awaken again.

Getting to your resolution is like mountain climbing. You can get to the top only one step at a time, and it will take thousands of steps to get there. It's easy to get discouraged when you get tired or stumble, but your compassionate, curious and committed mindset will help you return to your hope and proceed.[13] The view from the top will be worth it.

While determination harnesses our inspiration to push forward, it also needs to be balanced by flexibility. Sometimes when we analyze the setback, we discover the resolution needs to be modified or the goal isn't really one we want to pursue. Some obstacles are insurmountable or just bigger than we want to deal with. But most aren't. *Usually the barriers are just invisible until we bang into them.* Once the obstacle is revealed, we can find a path around and forward. It just takes determination and support to help us rally and move ahead.

Grow your determination by reminding yourself again and again why this resolution is important to you. Bring your awareness to the reasons your new behavior will enhance your life and how it is connected to your core identity and values.

Action-Able Exercise P5:
Elaborate your why

Think about why your new behavior matters. Pick two or three of the questions below to focus your thinking about the positive outcomes and hopes you have for your new habit. Your answers will illuminate the Destination part of your Habit Pathway—the rewards for your new action (Travel).

- When your new behavior is an ingrained habit, how will your life be different?
- How will you feel physically?
- Emotionally?

- How will your thoughts be different when your new habit is established?
- How will your new behavior affect your relationships?
- How will this change improve your life circumstances?
- What are the near-term benefits?
- How will your life be affected long-term?
- How is this new behavior an expression of your core personal/spiritual values?
- How is it an expression of your identity?

Write about your inspirations for making this change. Review and add to these notes regularly to support your determination and keep your inspiration for change top of mind.

Bring It All Together

To help you remember the details of your Action-Able Mindset, I'm going to stretch the rules of spelling:

Your Action-Able Mindset is:
Kompassionate
Inquisitive
and
Determined

I can hear your groan about my creative spelling, but since emotion makes things more memorable, I'm using your spelling irritation (or bemusement) to make my forced acronym stickier. Like the obnoxious jingle you can't get out of your head, but in this case, it's for a good cause, I promise!

If you really can't stand to spell compassion with a K, just remind yourself an Action-Able Mindset has 3 C's: Compassion, Curiosity and Commitment. But you can probably understand why I'd rather remind you to be KInD with yourself to support your Action-Ability.

To make this concept more helpful, imagine you have two companions on your journey: your KInD Coach and the Inner Critic. Your KInD Coach embodies your Action-Able Mindset and walks by your side each step along the way, guiding you around the Inner Critic. Eventually, the Inner Critic will fade and become less disruptive, but it won't disappear altogether.

Pause for a moment here to picture them one at a time as characters in an internal movie.

Start with the Inner Critic: Male or female? Tall or short? What does the Inner Critic look like? What is the Inner Critic holding or wearing? Give your Inner Critic a distinctive feature so s/he is easily recognized. For example, maybe s/he holds a magnifying glass to show how the Inner Critic zeros in on perceived flaws. Or it could be a gavel to show that the Inner Critic condemns you with judgment. Or maybe the Inner Critic always wears an orange sweater for no particular reason but that the bright color helps you spot him/her. It doesn't have to be complicated or symbolic, just some type of marker so you can easily tell who's who, differentiating the Inner Critic from your KInD Coach. Let your imagination create an image to go with the voice in your head.

In Action-Able Exercise P1, you wrote down what the Inner Critic says to you when you falter. Now consider how these words sound. Does s/he yell or use an insidious whisper or some other tone to communicate disapproval? What other details do you notice about the Inner Critic?

Picturing the Inner Critic enables your brain to experience it as outside of you, as externalized.[14] This way you can interact with your Inner Critic as separate from yourself rather than being inhabited by him/her. Disown the harsh inner voice.

Next, imagine your KInD Coach in great detail. Again: Male or female? Tall or short? What does your KInD Coach look like? What is s/he wearing or holding that helps you identify him/her with a quick glance? Maybe your KInD Coach is holding a staff to show her/his stability and wisdom. Or wears a luminous heart-shaped pendant to emphasize compassion. My KInD Coach wears hiking boots to remind me she's ready to stay with me as we trek across rocky terrain. Pause and see your KInD Coach.

You discovered the KInD Coach's words of encouragement in Action-Able Exercise P2 when you thought about how you would support a friend who feels discouraged. How does the KInD Coach use body language, tone of voice and supportive words to express warmth and encouragement?

When your KInD Coach asks questions to discover what went wrong during a setback, how will s/he convey compassionate curiosity? What will your KInD Coach say and do to activate your determination?

When you picture your KInD Coach as outside of yourself, externalized, you will experience him/her as distinct from your discouraged self. Imagine visiting with your KInD Coach, having a cup of coffee together or going for a walk. You can discuss why your goal is important and how to persevere around the obstacles.

You can imagine an internal scene where there are three characters: your discouraged self, your KInD Coach and the Inner Critic. As you hear your internal dialogue, identify who's talking. You can sideline the Inner Critic without argument. Give your KInD Coach more lines. *The KInD Coach ignores the Inner Critic* and focuses on connecting with your discouraged self to reawakening your curiosity and commitment.

When you're struggling, exhale slowly and invite your KInD Coach forward. Like Miranda regrouping in the parking lot, calming your body helps focus your mind so you can better understand the challenge at hand and restore your determination.

A Keystone Habit is a foundational habit that opens the door to other healthy behaviors.[15] For example, exercise is a keystone habit, because when people exercise they also tend to sleep better, make healthier eating choices, drink less, etc. Exercise unlocks the door and lets in the other healthy habits.

Similarly, developing the routine of exhaling and thinking of your KInD Coach empowers you to handle setbacks and live your best intentions in any area you choose. The keystone habit of the Action-Ability Approach is to exhale to calm your body and shift to your KInD Mind.

I used this keystone habit countless times to persist as I created this book for you. The sheer scope of this project felt overwhelming and discouraging at times. How will I wrestle all of these ideas into a useful process? How can I translate the dry scientific writing of my training to a more engaging, compelling style? How can I hear the constructive criticism of my early readers and find confidence to keep working to make it better? I need to persist because that's what I'm asking you to do. But when I feel daunted, it's hard to keep at it. I exhale and find my KInD Coach. She re-Fuels me by reminding me why this project matters and helps me find a micro-action to take the next step. I hear the voice of one of my favorite authors describing writing a book as like an ant eating an oak tree—you can do it only one bite at a time. This is a normal writer's challenge. Feeling connected re-energizes me. I can do this. Time for my next bite.

Miranda's KInD Coach is a beautiful, voluptuous woman. Her luminous brown eyes are warm and comforting, and she exudes confidence in herself and in Miranda. She's holding a kaleidoscope shimmering with vibrant colors, reminding Miranda that her KInD Coach is inquisitive and will look at her situation from lots of directions, to help Miranda see new possibilities. Her coach points the kaleidoscope at a bowl of colorful cut fruit, inviting Miranda to look through the lens to see food in new ways. Together, they point the kaleidoscope at the Inner Critic, seeing him in small fragments. Miranda spots the measuring tape he's holding, knowing he wants to size her up. She spins the kaleidoscope and smiles at her KInD Coach.

Miranda makes a decoration for her dining room to keep her KInD Coach nearby. She finds a crystal prism to remind her to look at her situation from lots of angles. She lights a candle and watches the light play through the crystal while she does her slow breathing. The candle's warmth reminds Miranda to be compassionate with herself. She adds a heart-shaped rock to remember the connection, emotional stability and self-love she is gaining, strengthening her determination to eat in a fun and healthy way.

Action-Able Exercise P6:
See your KInD Coach and Inner Critic

Create images of your KInD Coach and Inner Critic. The goal is to externalize these parts of yourself so you can *see* them.

You might do a simple sketch or drawing. If your Inner Critic picks at your artistic abilities, briefly notice this judgmental chatter and come back to your drawing. This exercise is not about creating artistic masterpieces. If writing is more comfortable for you than drawing, write a very detailed visual description of these parts so you can clearly see them in your mind's eye. Another option is to Google key words that describe these parts to find images online. For example, if the Inner Critic is a judge, search online to find judge images and pick one with a scowling expression. If the image doesn't have a gavel, cut and paste one onto the image. Collage the details you imagine together into an image that helps you see your Inner Critic clearly.

What does your Inner Critic look like? What are her/his identifying features? Use speech bubbles, like you would find in a comic strip, showing what the Inner Critic says. Create a vivid image by drawing, writing or finding online images so you see the Inner Critic.

Next see your KInD Coach. What is s/he wearing or holding? What does your KInD Coach say to encourage you? Capture this image by drawing, writing or collaging a detailed vision of your KInD Coach.

Full disclosure—I hate doing artistic exercises like this. But this activity kept pushing its way back into the Action-Ability Approach even when I tried to delete it. Then I sketched my inner parts, and it was transformative for me. When I drew my Inner Critic, I saw her clearly for the first time. She's the old-fashioned stereotype of a dowdy, scolding librarian, wearing glasses with her hair pulled back in a tight bun. My simple sketch of her says it all. She's watching vigilantly for my misdeeds, with her finger pointing out, ready to reprimand me. A breakthrough for my goal to stop nagging came when I spotted my Inner Critic turned outward, pointing her finger at my loved ones. I realized that when I'm struggling the most, I become the Critic. Yikes! Now I see this part of me and I work with my KInD Coach to manage my Inner Critic and keep her away from my family.

Picturing your inner conflicts in this way, even just in your imagination, will give you more information and a science-based solution for handling your internal struggle.

With your Action-Able Mindset, you have a plan to handle the biggest risk factor for giving up: feeling discouraged. By developing your keystone habit—exhaling to access your KInD Mind—you become emotionally prepared to live your best intentions.

Chapter Recap

♦ Feeling discouraged—losing hope—is the most common obstacle on the path to behavior change.

♦ The Action-Able Mindset is the foundation of all lasting change because it offers a way to transform discouragement into grit for sustained action.

♦ The Action-Able Mindset is compassionate, curious and committed to your goal.

- Self-compassion and forgiveness empower you to keep going after a slip-up.

- By being inquisitive rather than critical, you will notice details about the situation you overlooked before.

- Determination harnesses your hope and energizes you to follow through on your commitment to yourself. Fuel your determination by keeping the rewards for your work front and center.

- The Action-Able Mindset is a KInD Mind that is Kompassionate, Inquisitive and Determined. Envisioning your KInD Coach will help you strengthen this supportive inner experience.

- Picturing the Inner Critic as externalized helps you disown the negative chatter in your head and make more space for the KInD Coach.

- The practice of exhaling and imagining your KInD Coach is the keystone habit that opens the door to your new habit. This mental preparation empowers you to persist through the inevitable setbacks you will face.

Key Words

Action-Able Mindset, KInD Coach, Inner Critic

Your Cast of Characters

It's almost showtime. Let's find our seats. Imagine we're at the theater, getting settled to watch the performance. The curtain goes up and the stage is crowded with cast members for the opening number of *Change, the musical.* On the stage, you see the people in your life, costumed in green and red: supporters wear varying shades of green (for Go), and the unsupportive people you know are dressed in shades of red (for Stop). Your KInD Coach and Inner Critic are also on stage, as well as some other characters you don't recognize—we'll meet them soon. At the center of it all is the Hero. The tension of the scene builds as each cast member tugs the Hero in different directions, vying for control.

Watching the show, we see right away why it can be so challenging to change. Just as our KInD Coach supports our progress and our Inner Critic interferes, people we know can either help or disrupt progress toward our goals.[1]

When we're surrounded by people who share our healthy intentions, it's much easier to succeed with the group and follow through on our plans.[2] Programs like Alcoholics Anonymous, Weight Watchers, CrossFit and Meetup are impactful mainly because they bring people together who share common hopes. We learn from each other while offering and receiving the support we need to persist. Taking a yoga class, joining a faith community, going to a meditation group, finding an online community—all of these social situations can create connection and support our success.

However, the people in our life can also derail us from pursuing our goals. If changing our behavior has social costs and we feel more disconnected when we move toward our goal, it will be difficult to stay on track. Plus we are more likely to give up if our friends discourage our progress or engage in a behavior we are trying to stop. "I have never seen someone consistently stick to positive habits in a negative environment," observes the author of *Atomic Habits,* James Clear.[3]

We need a KInD Coach internally, but we also need to surround ourselves with people who are KInD. Who are the people in your life who offer an attitude of compassion, curiosity and commitment to help you persevere when you're struggling? Do your friends practice KInDness? How about your work supervisor? Your family members? Therapist? Faith leader? Fitness coach? Assess the cast of characters around you and orient toward those who will encourage and support you.

Also practice being a KInD Coach for your loved ones. If you're supporting your child who's struggling with home-work, be compassionate and curious as you assist your child in identifying the barriers to success, and be persistent in helping him/her problem-solve these challenges.

Miranda treats her cousin with KInDness when Yolanda asks how she's lost weight. Miranda offers encouragement and tells her about discovering CassidyEats. Based on Cassidy's recommendation, they decide to check out Weight Watchers together. Miranda and Yolanda download the WW app and explore the tips and recipes. Using the connect feature, they find other people who are grappling with food issues. Even Oprah uses WW to successfully manage her weight. Yolanda feels a spark of hope.

Kanesha would register them for a marital enrichment workshop at church in a second, but Marcus isn't interested in talking with other people about his marriage. He is private and introverted. The relationship book works better for him. He likes reading the stories of other men working to improve their marriages. Marcus doesn't have to interact with other people to learn from their experience—he can experience support and gain their wisdom through reading.

Rachel can't imagine talking with anyone about how she lashes out at Jason, but her grandmother has always been supportive. As a child, Rachel stayed with Nana when things were especially chaotic at home. Now Nana has dementia and lives nearby in a nursing home. Rachel goes for her usual visit with Nana. This time, instead of just holding Nana's hand while they watch TV together, Rachel talks to Nana in a whisper, tears streaming down her face. Nana's mind is gone so she doesn't know what Rachel is saying, but even so, Rachel knows Nana loves her no matter what. Nana's kind eyes gaze at Rachel and her pain eases a bit. It's a relief to say these things out loud. Maybe, just maybe, Rachel wonders, could she email the therapist she found online?

Who are the supportive people in your life? Orient to these special people and ask them to encourage the change you are working on. For example, my family, friends and colleagues helped me with this project, reading earlier versions of the book, showing me how to make it better and better with each draft. (Don't be fooled by a single author's name on the cover of a book. It takes a village to write a good book.)

You can also ask your friends to serve as accountability partners to encourage follow-through on your micro-resolutions. This has been the linchpin of my exercise routine. Countless times I've rallied when feeling too tired, busy or unmotivated to work out because my friend depends on me to show up. Our heart-to-heart talks are what really motivate me to drag myself to the gym.

In the Preparation Phase of habit development, surround yourself with supportive people. You don't need to cut out negative people; instead, focus your attention on the KInD people you know and on developing relationships with new supportive people.

As Miranda and Yolanda did when they joined WW, look for existing communities that support your resolution. If you have time to add a group or class, these can be highly impactful. If time is tight or you're introverted, there are online support programs and social apps for any goal you can imagine, creating easy access to community. Also consider finding a coach or therapist to guide you. By surrounding yourself with people who share your goals, you prepare the social environment for success.

Action-Able Exercise P7:
Assess your current social environment

Make a list of your current cast of characters. Who are the people with whom you have daily contact? Your family members, friends, coworkers, etc. Who are the other important people in your life? Even if you don't have regular contact with them, add their names to your list. Consider your other influencers, including authors, speakers, celebrities, or people in your community whom you're inspired by, even if you don't know them well.

Next, rate the level of support from each of these people for your making this change on a scale from -10 (totally unsupportive) to 0 (neutral) to +10 (enthusiastically supportive). Each person gets a rating. The friend who is your running partner might get a +10. Your sister who makes snarky comments about your fitness efforts might get a -5. The creator of the YouTube video who inspired you to take action in the first place could be rated a +8. Your coworker who doesn't know about your aspiration gets a 0 (neutral).

Level of support can be hard to rate for people who are encouraging one day and undermining the next. Note these people by indicating the range of their support. For example, if your sister is critical one day and nice the next, her rating might be -5 to +5.

Write the support ratings next to the names you listed above.

Next, scale your community by placing the names of your cast of characters on this continuum so you can see your current social environment more clearly. Do this task in pencil so you can move people around as their support levels change.

A support array might look like this:

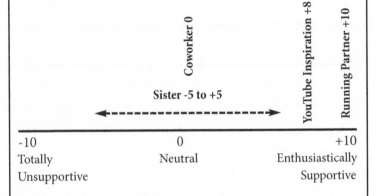

Take your ratings from the list above and show your community's range of support by plotting each person on the line below.

Support levels of my cast of characters:

-10	0	+10
Totally	Neutral	Enthusiastically
Unsupportive		Supportive

If the people in your life cluster toward the negative or neutral end of the scale, then preparation is urgently needed to build a positive community to support your goals. Think back to anyone who has been supportive in your past, as Rachel did with her grandmother. Draw on these KInD people and remember how you felt cared about. Use that feeling to find the courage to reach out for more support. Like Miranda, you might start online to find others sharing about similar struggles and remind you you're not alone. Find videos and books about your challenge to draw ideas and inspiration.

If your support graph shows a broader range, with people spanning from unsupportive to supportive, then bring your awareness to the people on the plus side of the continuum.

Also think about what could move each person up on the support scale. For people who are hovering near zero, do they know about your goal for change? For those who are likely to be supportive if they knew, tell them about your resolution and ask for their help.

Consider requesting that your loved ones with the highest support ratings write an encouraging letter, email or text (take a screen shot of the text) or to make a short video to remind you why your goal is important and help you keep going after you stumble. Ask someone to be your accountability partner.

Miranda makes a photo collage of the loved ones who are encouraging her new relationship with food. She asked them to write short notes to her, cheering her on, and she arranges these love notes with their photos. She hangs this collage up in the kitchen so her community keeps her company while she cooks. She can feel their support when she needs it the most.

Revisit Action-Able Exercise P7 to update your community as it evolves. Add new names to your support graph. Change the ratings as people become more or less supportive. If your running partner gets injured, her support level might go down while she's recovering. Or if your sobriety annoys your old drinking buddy, he might try to coax you back into drinking, revealing that his rating is even lower than you first thought.

When you feel discouraged, bring to mind someone who will be happy for your success. When you're not sure how to regroup after a setback, text someone on the plus side of your community.

Preparation of a strong social environment is crucial to support your Action Ability. By strengthening the encouragement from your existing community and getting to know new KInD people, you surround the Hero with as many characters in green as possible. The unsupportive characters in red will still be on the stage, but they will be outnumbered.

Your Inner Cast of Characters

In addition to the people who can support or disrupt your progress, you have an Internal cast of characters who clash, encouraging and discouraging your best and worst intentions. We've already explored two of these characters: the Inner Critic and the KInD Coach. But there are other inner players on the stage having an impact on the Hero.

The debates in your head are between these inner parts. Imagine the classic scene of the person with an angel on one shoulder and a devil on the other, each arguing its case. What's happening here? Why do we have these inner conflicts?

These clashes happen because of how the brain is designed. During brain evolution, "the system of self-control was slapped on top of the old system of urges and instincts," explains psychologist Kelly McGonigal.[4] This leaves us with a brain that has the driver upfront, our brain's logical frontal lobes, trying to stay on course while struggling to manage the rowdy passengers in the back of the bus, the hindbrain's compelling survival instincts. This biology leads to our experience of inner conflict.

To get a better handle on these power struggles, let's identify the cast of internal characters who are fighting for control over the Hero.

In addition to your Inner Critic and KInD Coach, notice your Tempted Self. This is the part of you who craves the forbidden experience. The neurochemical driving the Tempted Self is dopamine, which is central to how the brain harnesses attention and motivation. Dopamine is often thought of as creating the experience of reward or pleasure, but in fact what dopamine creates is craving—anticipation of the desired experience. By focusing on wanting something we don't yet have, dopamine generates tension to propel us forward.

If your resolution is to redirect an obsessive behavior, then you know how it feels when the Tempted Self drips dopamine into your system. This urge Fuels your Travel in the wrong direction, where you drink too much, shop compulsively or gamble past the limit you were trying to hold. My Tempted Self craves the calm I feel after I micromanage my kids.

Miranda knows her Tempted Self uses sweets to coax her off course, while Yolanda has to watch out for her Tempted

Self especially when she smells freshly baked bread. Rachel's Tempted Self agitates her with seemingly righteous anger and a distorted belief that she's dispensing justice. As she rages at Jason, she feels relief from the tension of holding in her anger, which momentarily rewards her aggressiveness. When I'm itching to nag, my Tempted Self teams up with the Critic, egging me on, saying I'm being negligent if I don't unleash my know-it-all. What Fuels your Tempted Self?

Seeing the Tempted Self more clearly empowers you to better manage cravings and maintain your commitment to your resolution.

Action-Able Exercise P8:
See your Tempted Self

Imagine your Tempted Self and create a simple picture using images or words to help you see this character clearly. Focus on the distinctive features so you can tell who's who. How will you tell the difference between the Inner Critic and the Tempted Self?

Again, decide about gender. Does Your Tempted Self loom over you in height, or is it small and mischievous? What is your Tempted Self holding or wearing? How can you show the dopamine-fueled anticipation? There might be drool involved or something else to show its intense emotion. Use a speech bubble to show what the Tempted Self says to provoke your lapse.

Sketch, write or collage online images to see your Tempted Self clearly.

Your Manager is the character battling with the Tempted Self. The Manager lives in the frontal lobes of your brain. This part of you sees the future benefits of your goal, makes a plan, organizes you to get there and helps you keep a grip emotionally so you stay on course.

The Manager's actions are crucial for creating lasting change. In their book, *Smart but Scattered Guide to Success*, psychologists Peg Dawson and Richard Guare describe the self-management skills people need to live their best intentions.[5] These include time management, organization, sustaining attention, planning and prioritizing, coping with distraction, resisting temptation and persistence. Some people are more naturally organized than others, but self-management skills can be learned and strengthened. For example, your keystone habit of slow breathing quiets the Tempted Self and activates your Manager.

You don't need to fight with your Tempted Self to prevent a lapse. You just need to spot your Tempted Self in action, exhale and shift your focus to your KInD Coach and Manager. Your slow breathing wakes up your brain's frontal lobes and enables you to connect with the Manager's signature Pause and Plan Response, which is essential for willpower.[6]

Action-Able Exercise P9:
See your Manager

Imagine your Manager. Is your Manager male or female? What's your Manager wearing or holding? My Manager carries a clipboard, showing me she's organized and has a plan. A heart is drawn on the back of her clipboard, reminding me my Manager is nice, not a taskmaster like the Inner Critic. How will you see your Manager's calm thoughtfulness? What does your Manager say to keep you focused on your goal?

Create a detailed image of your Manager.

While the Tempted Self is obvious and openly provocative, the Saboteur is a sneaky character intent on slipping past your Manager and undoing your progress. Catch the Saboteur by looking for its trademark thought pattern—rationalization. Misusing your progress as a reason to take it easy, the Saboteur reassures by saying, "You had a healthy lunch. It's fine to have a yummy dessert." When the voice in your head says some version of "I've been so good. I deserve to take a break," you know the Saboteur is in action.[7] The Saboteur usually works in pluses and minuses that leave us at zero, undoing our progress.

The Saboteur offers the temptation as the reward. This is referred to as the Halo Effect. The progress you've made is used by the Saboteur to put a halo onto the temptation, disguising your inner devil to look like an angel.[8] "I saved so much money on the sale so I can buy this extra thing."

Beware! The Saboteur disguises itself as the KInD Coach, often using an encouraging voice to relieve your guilt, giving you permission to lapse and justifying your missteps. But know this: Your KInD Coach would never lead you astray.

Your KInD Coach or Manager might offer you a reward or treat, but it will never be in the form of temptation. The best rewards support the change goal. When you finish a difficult project, you might reward yourself with a celebratory meal with one of your favorite coworkers. You can also use treats to refill your energy reserve.[9] Treats are unearned, specifically not associated with your progress—this stops the Saboteur from trading treats for progress. After an especially draining week, you might treat yourself with a massage. The purpose of the treat is to restore and refresh you. The forbidden item or experience is never used as a treat.

Your KInD Coach and Manager will maintain your goal focus, reminding you why it matters to stay the course. This is why the KInD Coach's determination is essential. Keeping a high level of commitment to the goal blocks the Saboteur's attempts to use your progress against you. Return to your answers in Action-Able Exercise R1 "I want to, because" and P5, where you elaborated why you are working on this goal. Reduce the Saboteur's power by focusing on your commitment.

Miranda knows her Saboteur well. She sees his smiling mask and watches him borrow the Inner Critic's measuring tape. When she slims down a bit, the Saboteur coaxes her to celebrate with a sweet treat. But she knows better. Miranda reminds herself her goal is to gain a healthy relationship with food rather than over-focusing on losing pounds and inches. When she wants to treat herself, she buys herself the new kitchen gadget she has been eyeing.

Like any devious disrupter, once spotted, the Saboteur switches tactics. Another signature trick performed by the Saboteur is to use your Future Self to derail your progress. When it's challenging to follow through on our resolutions today, the Saboteur reassures us that the conditions tomorrow, next week or next month will be easier so we can start our change plan later. Our Today Self is off the hook because the Future Self will do it.

In contrast, the KInD Coach will help you understand why the next step feels hard to do now and will strategize about how to clear the obstacles as soon as possible, probably today, in order to keep you on track. The KInD Coach never encourages inaction—that's when you know the Saboteur is talking. Rather, your KInD Coach will help you find a micro-action you can do today to maintain your forward momentum.

The Saboteur also uses the promise of your healthy Future Self to justify a last hurrah. The voice of the Saboteur is in your head when, right before the date you plan to start living your resolution, you go on a drinking or eating binge or spending spree. Although this can seem celebratory or encouraging, the "one-last-time" approach isn't KInD, and it lowers the odds of success.

The Saboteur is also the voice behind the What-the-Hell Effect. When you have a lapse, the voice in your head says, "Screw it. I can't do this anyway. I might as well enjoy myself fully." Disengaging from the resolution, the Saboteur amps up the Tempted Self and works to steer your awareness away from your goal.[10]

Action-Able Exercise P10:
See your Saboteur

How will you spot the Saboteur? Consider the usual questions as you see this sneaky character. What is your Saboteur wearing or holding to help you identify him/her? Maybe your Saboteur wears an old-fashioned spy's fedora and trench coat with the collar up as he tries to hide himself. Or maybe she's a double agent wearing sunglasses. Use a cartoon speech bubble to show what your Saboteur says to upend your progress.

Create a detailed image of your Saboteur so you can clearly see him/her in your mind's eye.

Your Future Self doesn't want to be co-opted by the Saboteur—it's an ally of your Manager and KInD Coach. Your Future Self is the grateful recipient of your commitment to lasting change.

When we think about the impact of our current actions on our Future Self, we're more likely to stick with our best intentions.[11] For example, imagining our Future Self enjoying the benefits of today's financial responsibility can inspire us to save for our later years. Financial planners sometimes show their clients a photo of what they might look like at 80 years old to create a stronger Future Self connection, and it improves retirement savings rates.[12] Feeling connected to your Future Self amplifies your awareness of the long-term rewards of your new habit.

The advice to "dress for the job you want" also harnesses the inspiration of the Future Self. You can wear the clothing of your Future Self now to support your new habit. This usually refers to dressing professionally, but it could also mean wearing workout clothes as a reminder that you are someone who will exercise today.

Gretchen Rubin, the author of *The Happiness Project* and *Better Than Before*, calls on a positive relationship with her Future Self when she coaches herself to "act the way I want to feel."[13] What can we do now to make our Future Self feel calmer, happier, more energetic, more confident, etc.?

Maybe we have a resolution about taking more risks socially. Usually we let the emotion drive the action: "I don't feel confident enough to go to the party. When I feel better about myself, I'll go to parties." Instead, by letting your Future Self direct the scene, your courageous actions create the emotion you're seeking.[14] When you adopt Rubin's rule and act the way you *want* to feel, you go to the party and act like a confident person: think of an ice breaker question ahead of time, exhale to calm yourself and approach someone new to start a conversation. These actions build confidence.

Action-Able Exercise P11:
See your Future Self

As the curtain rises on Act 2 of our show, the story has jumped ahead in time, and we see your Future Self thriving. We don't yet know how this transformation occurred, but it's clear you are happy and healthy, doing your new habit with ease.

Let the scene unfold, witnessing your Future Self in action.[15] How do you recognize this character as your Future Self, distinct from the Hero who is struggling to change? What does your Future Self think, feel and do differently now that your new habit is well established? What does your Future Self wear or hold to show this transformation?

Create a detailed image of your Future Self.

Having watched your Future Self in action, you can now put yourself into the scene. When you aren't sure how to move toward your resolution, select a Future Self action and go for it. Though you might believe you need to feel and think differently, the reverse is true.[16] *Emotions and thoughts change after we've changed our behavior, not the other way around.*† When we try to shift the feelings and thoughts first, we get stuck waiting and don't act. Let your Future Self call you forward to action.

Rachel's Future Self is patient. She sees her Future Self using prayer beads, drawing on a spiritual connection to shift from frustration to calm. This reminds Rachel of Nana's daily routine of saying the rosary. Even though her grandmother's

---

† Clinical depression, anxiety and ADHD sometimes require medication before behavior change is possible. By changing the neurochemistry with medication, thoughts and feelings shift and make previously inaccessible actions possible.

Catholic practice doesn't feel right for her, Rachel sees her Future Self using a similar string of beads as she prays for patience. She watches her Future Self wrap the beads around her wrist when she's done with her prayers, touching the beads throughout the day to stay centered.

The journey from hope to habit involves bridging the gap between our current identity as someone who *wants* to change and our goal identity as someone who *has* changed. "Every action you take is a vote for the type of person you wish to become," explains change expert James Clear.[17] The votes don't have to be unanimous, but the identity with the most votes (actions) wins. The Saboteur works to suppress votes for change. But now your Manager and KInD Coach can spot the Saboteur in action and empower you to vote for your healthy Future Self.

Clear points out that the root of the word *identity* means "repeated being-ness."[18] We become what we do over and over again. Act as who you want to be—embody your Future Self now. Live your hope.

Action-Able Exercise P12:
Gratitude from the future

Write a gratitude letter to your Today Self from the perspective of your Future Self. Thank your Today Self for doing the work to create this positive future.

When I did this exercise, I burst into tears, surprised and comforted by how tender my Future Self was toward me in my struggle to stop micromanaging. She understands how fear about my mother's illness grips me as a parent, especially now that my son has the same illness. My Future Self holds my core emotional wound while reminding me how resilient my children, my mother and I are. Her letter reassured me that no matter where life takes us all, we will be OK. My Future Self appreciates how scary it is for me to let go and how I vulnerable I feel when taking the steps to bring her into being.

Your Future Self needs you. S/he won't exist without your healthy action today.

———— • ————

Now you have the cast of inner characters identified: your KInD Coach and your Inner Critic, your Tempted Self and your Manager, your Saboteur and your Future Self. Imagine them on the stage, supportive parts dressed in green and disrupters in red.

While the people in your life might switch between red and green, becoming more or less supportive, *your internal parts cannot switch sides.* Your negative inner parts have only one way of operating, dictated by biology. The Tempted Self swims in dopamine and lives in the hindbrain so it can only impulsively pursue desire. (Although the writers on the children's show *Sesame Street* tried to rewrite Cookie Monster into a healthy eating advocate, nobody was fooled!)

The Inner Critic is only disapproving, the Tempted Self always opposes self-discipline, and the Saboteur always undermines progress. On the other hand, if your Manager seems to become frustrated with your struggle to prepare for your resolution, then you know the Inner Critic has disguised him/herself as your Manager. The Manager is always and only encouraging.

As we proceed, you will learn how to usher these disruptive parts off stage, yet they won't go away. The Inner Critic, Tempted Self and Saboteur wait in the wings, watching for a chance to jump back into the action and upset your progress. But now that you know how they operate, your Manager is on duty and can keep the negative parts out of the spotlight.

During the Preparation Phase, the internal work is to strengthen the KInD Coach, Manager and Future Self and their relationship to the Hero, creating a positive inner social environment.

Let's start with a pre-assessment, rating the strength of the supportive and disruptive inner parts, to clarify the preparation needed to set the stage for success.

Action-Able Exercise P13:
Assess your internal social environment

Now that you can see your cast of inner characters, rate their levels of support for you at the start of your change journey.

The KInD Coach, Manager and Future Self are, by definition, positive. Rate the strength of their encouragement by assigning a number from +1 (slightly supportive) to +10 (enthusiastically supportive). For example, if you feel inspired by your vision of a better life once your new behavior is well established, then your Future Self is fairly strong, maybe a +8. However, the development of your KInD Coach might not be as strong yet since it's a newer concept, so its rating might be a +4.

Rate the support of each positive part below:
KInD Coach: _____   Manager:_____   Future Self:_____

The Inner Critic, Tempted Self and Saboteur are, by definition, negative. Rate the power of their disruption by assigning a number from -1 (slightly unsupportive) to -10 (totally unsupportive). For example, if you were raised by harsh parents or suffer from depression, your Inner Critic might be especially strong, maybe a -9. If you're dealing with redirecting an obsessive behavior, your Tempted Self is probably strong, maybe a -7.

Rate each part below:
Inner Critic:_____   Tempted Self:_____   Saboteur:_____

Next, scale your inner parts by placing the names of your inner cast of characters on this continuum to see your current internal social environment more clearly. Use a pencil so you can move parts around as their support levels change in the future.

Note the boundary on this graph at zero. Unlike the people in our life, inner parts are not neutral. They are either positive or negative and cannot cross over.

For example, your internal support graph might look like this:

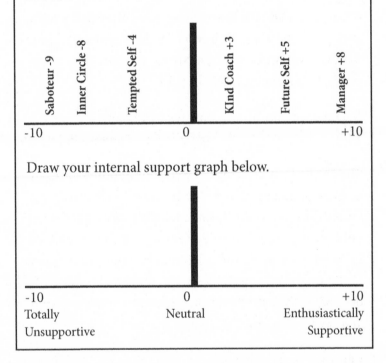

Draw your internal support graph below.

Seeing your internal parts strengthens your awareness of the positive inner parts and weakens the disrupters. Now as you listen to your self-talk, you know whose voice you hear.

There is no need to argue with the negative internal parts. The goal is to notice them, exhale and shift to connecting with the positive inner parts and the supportive people in your life.

The work of the Preparation Phase for the internal environment is to strengthen your encouraging parts. Inner support ratings of +5 or higher are needed for your positive parts to get you through the Sustained Action Phase. Take the time now to enhance your KInD Coach, Manager and Future Self.

Here is a list of the Action-Able Exercises identified by which positive inner part they support. Focus your preparation on completing or revisiting the exercises associated with the inner parts you most need to strengthen.

Exercise # strengthens this part:	KInD Coach	Manager	Future Self
R1: Pick your first potential resolution			X
R2: Explore your resolution challenge (Is it absent-minded, obsessive or avoidant?)	X		
R4: Two minutes of daily attention to slow breathing	X	X	
P2: How would you encourage your friend?	X		
P3: What sets you up for success?	X		X
P4: Reflect on HALT	X	X	
P5: Elaborate your why	X		X
P6: See your KInD Coach	X		
P9: See your Manager		X	
P11: See your Future Self			X
P12: Gratitude from the future			X
P13: Scale your internal social environment	X	X	

Watching *Change, the musical* reveals important insights into the social dynamics of your transformation process. Observe how the people in your life interact with your inner parts, collaborating for better and for worse. The supportive people amplify the power of the KInD Coach, Manager and Future Self. The unsupportive people Fuel the Inner Critic, Tempted Self and Saboteur. Watching these scenes play out, you discover important insights about your social environment.

The turning point happens when the Hero stops fighting with the negative people and inner parts, disregarding them, and moves forward, buoyed by a sea of supportive characters in green.

Chapter Recap

◆ Prepare your social environment to support your resolution.

◆ It's easier to change when you are surrounded by KInD people. Identify and develop new relationships with encouraging people. Ask for support and accountability. When you feel discouraged, bring to mind someone who will be happy for your success.

◆ Your social environment also includes internal parts battling for control over your behavior.

- The Tempted Self craves the forbidden experience. The neurochemical Fueling the Tempted Self is dopamine, which affects attention, motivation and anticipation.

- The Manager lives in the frontal lobes of your brain. This part of you sees the future benefits of your goal, makes a plan and organizes you to get there. The Manager's signature Pause and Plan Response is essential for willpower.

- The Saboteur tricks you into letting go of your resolution, rationalizing your lapses by pointing TO your progress as justification of giving in to temptation (Halo Effect). The Saboteur also procrastinates by assigning the goal to your Future Self so you never take action today.

- Treats can be used to restore and refresh you, but the forbidden item or experience is never used as a treat. That's when you know the Saboteur is trying to trick you.

- Your Future Self is the grateful recipient of your work for lasting change. When you think about the impact of your current actions on your Future Self, you're more likely to live your best intentions.

- Act the way you want to feel, embodying your Future Self to create the emotion you're seeking.

- ◆ There is no need to argue with the negative internal parts. The goal is to notice them, exhale and connect with the positive inner parts and supportive people in your life.

- ◆ During the Preparation Phase, enhance your inner social environment by strengthening the KInD Coach, Manager and Future Self. Prepare your outer social environment by fostering your relationships with positive people in your life.

Key Words

KInD people, Manager, Future Self, Tempted Self, Saboteur

You Are the Hero

While the stage is crowded with your cast of characters, one matters more than any others: you, the Hero. You are the one who does the work to create lasting change. As with any Hero's journey, there are trials and tribulations, lessons and triumphs. Negative inner parts and people will obstruct you and try to lead you astray. Encouraging people and your positive inner parts will help you find a way through, but each forward step of the journey is made by you.

To best prepare, identify your own strengths and vulnerabilities before venturing forth to the Sustained Action Phase. *There is no one-size-fits-all solution for creating new habits.* What works for someone else might not work for you. What works when you're in one situation might not work when the situation changes. We're most successful when we design a personalized approach that best fits our tendencies.[1]

Jasmin is motivated by other people's opinions. Now that her nails have grown out, she has fun trying to get people to notice her hands. She paints her nails bright red. Jasmin's excited about her sister Samira's upcoming wedding and the Mehendi ceremony where their hands will be decorated with henna tattoos.

Miranda feels discouraged when she thinks about other people's opinions. Though she's happy about having lost 34 pounds so far, she accepts she will never be a skinny mini—she's just not built like that. Miranda's mad about the cruelty and discrimination heavier people like her face. She wants to opt out of thinking about weight altogether.

Marcus is an introvert and Kanesha is a ravenous extrovert. They're a great match because he is content to listen while she's happy to talk, especially now that she can tell he's listening. Kanesha spends lots of time away from home, socializing with her many friends. That's fine with Marcus. It gives him plenty of time to himself. He's happily occupied with his woodworking and welding projects. Marcus loses track of time, crafting an elaborate garden sculpture for one of Kanesha's friends. Marcus and Kanesha's differences work for them.

But sometimes we feel like a round peg trying to fit into a square hole. That's how Jamal feels at work. His coworkers thrive in their open-office setup, but he can't think straight. All the noise and chatter distract him. Plus, whenever he finally gets his thoughts flowing, a coworker comes over to get his input about a new project. He wishes his coworkers would stop interrupting him. Jamal realizes he probably needs to say something, but just thinking about that makes him really anxious. Last week, he got his nerve up to ask his supervisor if he could work from home, but she said no. Now he turns his attention back to the monitors. Jamal tries to remember where he left off. He slips on his noise-canceling headphones, hoping to ignore the next interruption.

Like Jamal, I struggled to find a work approach that fit for me. I'd been trying to set up a daily writing routine, because it seemed to be the habit of most professional writers. But my schedule as a parent and therapist just didn't give me a manageable daily window for writing. And at that time, I was too tired to get up earlier or stay up later to make time each day to write, so I wasn't working on the book at all.

I'd almost decided to let the project go, but then my youngest child left for college and my life circumstances changed. My schedule was still too irregular to find a standard time each day for writing, so instead I came up with a micro-resolution I knew I could stick with. I committed to write at least 30 minutes every Sunday morning. This easy action opened the floodgates. Once I started writing at least weekly, I had the book project on my mind all the time, and soon I was writing most days, often for hours at a time.

Also, I discovered that writing this book for you was the secret to making progress on my micromanaging resolution. My obsessively worried mind needed distraction. Turns out noodling about the Action-Ability Approach was the perfect shiny object for me to focus on to direct me away from micromanaging my kids.

What about your resolution? Consider your unique personality, tendencies and circumstances to prepare a work-able plan for your situation. Then, as you proceed, work with your inquisitive KInD Coach to learn more about yourself and your circumstances to modify your plans as needed.

Remember Action-Able Exercise P3, where you were invited to explore what sets you up for success. When we look at our successes, we identify the situations that work well with who we are and how we operate in general. For example, if you're a morning person and the yoga class you're interested in starts at 7a.m., you are more likely to get there than would someone who's a night owl. Fortunately, most yoga studios have classes throughout the day to offer opportunities for lots of people's circadian rhythms and life circumstances. And, if you're more introverted and prefer not to do activities in a group at all, then looking for online yoga videos will be a better fit for you.

Prepare a plan for your resolution that works with your natural inclinations.

Action-Able Exercise P14:
Get to know the Hero

Be self-reflective. Consider the following list of questions. Select the items relevant to your resolution to build your awareness about those issues. Down the road, if you get stuck, come back to the questions you're skipping today to see if there is another personal tendency you need to address.

- Are you more of a morning person or an evening person?
- Do you prefer to do a new activity with other people or on your own?
- Are you more introverted or extroverted?
- How much does the approval of others matter to you?

- Do expectations from others motivate you or activate rebelliousness?
- Are you more organized or disorganized?
- Do you tend to work in bursts or long hauls?
- Do you tend to start projects early or wait until the last minute?
- Do you prefer the excitement of starting a new activity or the experience of completion?
- Do you prefer the comfort of routine or the excitement of new experiences?
- Do you tend to seek out or avoid change?
- Is moderation easy for you or is it easier to abstain from a temptation altogether?
- Where do you have open time in your day? Where can you make time?
- What time of day is your mind sharpest? When is your willpower strongest?
- What healthy activities energize or refresh you?
- What are your quirks, unique tendencies or routines that this goal needs to work around?
- What atypical challenges do you grapple with?

Take notes about the tendencies relevant to your resolution.

The answers to these questions give you information about yourself and remind you to prepare interventions that work specifically for you.

Be skeptical of change methods promoted as *the* way to create your new habit. As humans, we are too diverse for the challenge of lasting change to have one simple solution. Customize your intervention. Having the wind at your back will ease your journey.

Consider your unique strengths and struggles when preparing your plan. For example, maybe you work a full-time job, then drive across town daily to visit an ailing parent, slogging along in heavy traffic, getting home late and exhausted. This stressful situation leaves little room to add the self-care activities crucial for staying healthy. You will have to think about where you tend to have the most energy and weave in micro-care activities to restore yourself. For example, you might decide to turn off the news radio and play calming music or talk by phone with a supportive friend during your drive time. You might find a tube of pleasant-smelling hand cream to calm your nervous system. Maybe you carve out a full hour at work for lunch and take a midday walk. Or do 10 minutes of deep exhalations anywhere in your day. These ideas work with the constraints of your situation.

Solving the problems of the mismatches between your personal tendencies and your situation requires creativity. Your KInD Coach brings inquisitiveness and determination to help the Hero find a path around each obstacle. Look for community with people who are similar to you in personality or circumstances to find new ideas for working through the issues you're facing.

As your KInD Coach cheers you on, tap into the most important personal strength of the Hero—the belief that you can change.[2] By following through on your easy micro-actions, you build your confidence that change is possible. By developing your keystone habit of exhaling and connecting with your KInD Coach, you open the door for your new behavior. You can feel even more hopeful now about living your best intentions because you are preparing a change plan just for you.

Action-Able Exercise P15:
See the Hero's strengths

Create an image of the Hero.

You can sketch or use a photo of yourself. Incorporate your answers to the above questions with short phrases or symbols. This image, surrounded by key words, enriches your awareness of your tendencies and strengths so you can prepare your own customized plan.

Chapter Recap

◆ There is no one-size-fits-all solution for creating new habits.

◆ We're most successful when we prepare a personalized approach that best fits our circumstances, tendencies, strengths and vulnerabilities.

◆ When we look at our successes, we identify the situations that work well with who we are and how we operate in general.

◆ The most important personal strength of the Hero is the belief that you can change. Success on your micro-resolutions creates confidence that change is possible.

Key Words

Customize

Set the Stage for Change

Turns out the secret to Miranda's success is meal planning. Now it's her Saturday morning routine. She discovered months ago that having a shopping list makes all the difference at the grocery store. Instead of wandering down the aisles, filling the cart with junk food like she used to, now she decides ahead of time what she will buy. Miranda knows just where to go to find what she needs and which aisles to steer clear of. She spends Saturday mornings on CassidyEats and the WW app, scrolling through recipes. Miranda plans her meals and snacks for the week and even figures in some sweets.

Since she lives by herself, this is easier for Miranda than it is for Yolanda, who's struggling to plan her meals while also feeding her family. Fortunately, Cassidy's recipes are good enough that even Yolanda's teenage kids like some of them. But the kids also want their comfort food, and lots of those recipes are off limits for Yolanda. Plus, her husband and kids want the shelves at home to be stocked like a 7-Eleven so they can grab a soda and chips or a candy bar anytime. Having all of those temptations at her fingertips makes Yolanda miserable. All day long, her mind battles with the Doritos in her cabinet. When her willpower runs out, she eats the whole party-size bag in one sitting.

Our Inner Critic is harsh when we buckle under the weight of temptation. "If you were really committed to your goal, you would resist! Either you're weak or you don't really want to change." But willpower is a limited resource.[1] As with gasoline in our car's tank, we can go only so far before we run out of willpower.

Resisting temptation takes a lot of energy. Lapses often happen later in the day, because we have spent all of our I-won't power earlier and have run out by evening.[2]

Help the Hero by empowering your Manager to prepare the physical environment and remove items that activate your Tempted Self. Eliminating temptations reduces the number of willpower struggles, so your energy is reserved for when you really need it.

Especially if you're struggling with an obsessive behavior, removing access to temptation is crucial. Eliminate your cigarettes, booze or cookies and put something else in their place. Remember Action-Able Exercise R3, translating Don't into I will. What did you decide to do instead? For example, *Don't smoke* becomes *I will chew gum*. Stock up on gum and put it where you usually keep your cigarettes. On autopilot, you will reach into your pocket for a cigarette and find a pack of gum in your hand, which will remind you of your resolution to stop smoking.

Preparing our environment to make the preferred choice easier is referred to as Choice Architecture.[3] By designing our surroundings to prevent temptation and support our resolution, we can set ourselves up for success. In Seattle, architects of the six-story Bullitt Center designed their building to encourage walking by building an "irresistible stairway" that draws people up and down the wide wooden staircase with bright windows and spectacular views.[4] The elevator is tucked away—out of sight, out of mind. Workers and visitors are much more likely to hit these inviting stairs than in a traditional office building.

Months ago, Miranda asked her boyfriend, Sergio, to come over and help clean out her kitchen. Together they went through her fridge and cabinets to get rid of the temptations. Miranda knew she would eventually eat them if they were in her home. Sergio took some of the things he likes to his house, and she threw the rest in the trash. Now Miranda stocks up on healthy food she likes and has a much easier time living her best intentions for eating.

How can you set up your environment to help you live your best intentions?

Your Manager's job is to get objects onto the stage in the right place, at the right time for the characters to perform their next scene. Examine your stage as it's currently set up. What items does the Hero need? What objects do the disruptive parts and people use to lead the Hero astray? Which items need to be taken off stage? Stored or thrown away? Notice the Saboteur encouraging you to keep a tempting item in the prop closet rather than putting it in the trash. Exhale and connect with your Manager to take charge and prepare your physical environment.

Set the stage for success. If the goal for stress management is to play the guitar at the end of a long day rather than watching TV, you could unplug your TV and put it away. Pull out your guitar and leave it on the couch where you usually sit to watch TV. By managing the props on your stage, you remind yourself of the resolution, making it easier to follow through. Now, as you go to plop on the couch ready to watch TV, you have to pick the guitar up because it's in the place you usually sit, and then the right prop is in your hand, in position for the intended scene where you relax by playing the guitar.

When we live with other people, preparing the environment is usually more challenging. Your family might object to the TV being moved to the closet. Let them know of your resolution and ask for a compromise. For example, maybe they'd be willing to drape a towel over the TV when they're done watching, so you have to pause to remove the cover, disrupting your autopilot, prompting you to make a more conscious choice.

Yolanda talks with her husband, Roger, about how hard it is for her to resist the junk food in their kitchen. He wants to support her but doesn't want to give up junk food himself, and neither of them wants to take on this battle with their kids. They decide to rearrange their kitchen cabinets and put Yolanda's snack food in an easily accessible cabinet near the sink and move their in-home 7-Eleven out of the way to the cabinets by the back door. This is still hard because Yolanda knows the back shelves are stocked with her favorite temptations, but at least she doesn't have to rummage through the junk food to find her snack. She's not sure if this will work, but it's worth a try.

Marcus doesn't need physical items for his new habit of talking more often. Instead, he collects words and has them ready when Kanesha pauses to let him chime in, showing her he's listening.

But now Marcus has a crisis on his hands. He rubs the growth he discovered in the deep tissue of his abdomen to make sure it's still there. It is. Is he imagining that it seems bigger? He needs to tell Kanesha, and he can't find the nerve to bring the subject up. He wishes Kanesha would just find it on her own, so he wouldn't have to say it, but it's not noticeable to her light, tender touch. The sentence "I found a lump" scares him to say out loud. If he tells Kanesha, she will make him talk to a doctor. He remembers his father's death after a long, difficult battle with cancer, and his jaw clenches.

Kanesha will be mad when she finds out he's known this long and hasn't said anything. The moment is never right. With each week that goes by, his tension builds, but this only makes it harder for the words to come out. Marcus realizes there's no way to make this conversation less awful—he just needs to say something.

We often seek the "right moment" to do the difficult thing, as if it will get easier later. The Saboteur urges you to delegate the unpleasant experience to the Future Self. Like a stage manager who handles timing cues so the characters know *what to do when*, have your Manager pick a specific date and time to go for it. For example, when people identify a specific date they plan to quit smoking, they are much more likely to succeed.[5]

In addition to a start date, we need to think through when our new habit will fit into our regular routine. Like my finding the right window of time for my weekly writing, figure out what will work best for your schedule and circumstances.

At the office, Jamal searches for the quiet times and discovers he can come in early before his coworkers arrive to start his day with two hours of uninterrupted work. Jamal's a morning person, so he's always up before dawn, and his supervisor doesn't care when he gets his work done as long as he's in the office.

Jamal is responsible for developing the company's digital marketing, implementing the barrage of ideas his coworkers come up with. They brainstorm nonstop content for the website, social media and targeted ads. Jamal can hardly handle the latest ideas before they come up with a new hot concept and send him in a different direction. He relishes his quiet mornings when he can concentrate on the programming details to complete yesterday's projects. Plus, he usually gets another hour or so to himself with his headphones on while his coworkers are settling in at the office before their creative juices really start flowing. But somewhere in the 10 o'clock hour, the first head peers over the wall of his cubicle. "Hey Jamal, we need you to. . ."

Just as preparing the physical environment is more challenging with other people in the mix, our social circumstances at home or work impact timing issues, too. Jamal discovered he can take advantage of the difference between him and his coworkers to capture time when he can get into a flow with his work. Finding the right timing given our unique tendencies and social situation can be tricky, so we often need to think outside the box. Jamal stepped out of the 9-to-5 box and I stepped out of the must-write-daily box to create customized solutions that work for each of us. It might take some trial and error to come up with the right timing for you. Work with your Manager to decide *when* to start your new action and *when* your new action will best fit into your routine.

Marcus knows tonight is the night. He spent the day crafting the awkward sentence that will shift the conversation to where he speaks rather than always listening. Kanesha has been sharing about office politics at the bank but notices Marcus is looking down at his hands instead of at her. She pauses, and Marcus reaches over, taking her hand. Confused, Kanesha's heart skips a beat. Marcus looks at her and forces the words out of his mouth. "Kanesha, honey, I've waited much longer than I should have to tell you this, but I couldn't figure out how to say it. I found a lump in my belly."

Rachel wears a string of green mala meditation beads wrapped around her wrist as a Sign to remind her to be patient. She likes the feeling of the cool stone beads and soft tassel. Rachel starts each day by doing her patience prayer for 10 minutes, which leaves her calmer during the morning routine with Jason. But evenings have been harder. Rachel's tired from her long nursing shifts at the hospital and usually comes home tapped out and irritable. This week, she's trying something new. When she gets home from work, she stays in her car in the driveway to do five more minutes of patience prayers before she goes into the house. As her fingers move across the beads, her faith perks her up, like a thirsty flower revived by a sprinkle of water.

Rachel's beads remind her to pause and collect herself before going into the house. What helps you remember your new activity?

A stage manager is in charge of cues, making sure the characters get on stage at the right time to start the scene. Work with your Manager to develop Signs to prompt the start of your new habit. Use technology (phones, watches) to set alarms or reminders. Or block out time on your calendar. Use Post-It notes. Make an artistic Sign. Create a customized screen saver or password for your devices reminding you of your resolution. For example, if you want to remember your Action-Able Mindset, you could make a computer password to prompt yourself to exhale and "Be KInD!"

Another solution for cueing a new action is to pair it with an existing habit.[6] For example, if you're trying to create the habit of taking a new medication each day, put your pill container next to your toothbrush so your well-established routine of brushing your teeth serves as a Sign to take your pills. However, most regular habits are done absent-mindedly, so you could easily brush your teeth without even noticing the pillbox. It can help to mix up the autopilot sequence a bit to activate your awareness. You could prepare your physical environment by putting your toothpaste on top of the pillbox and moving them both front and center on your counter.

An important trick for cueing your new action is to transform the trigger for the old behavior into a Sign pointing to your resolution. Habit expert Charles Duhigg describes this as the Golden Rule of Habit Change.[7] He emphasizes that an unhealthy habit will always lurk in the background, seeking an opening to return, but when you use the cue for the old behavior to remind you to do your new habit, it will be much easier to create lasting change. For example, recovering alcoholics learn to use the craving for a drink as a reminder to call a friend or go to an AA meeting. The urge to drink is included in the resolution Habit Pathway as a Sign for the new action. We've translated *Don't* into *I will*, and we can use the temptation for the unwanted action to remind us to do our resolution.

Rachel is vigilantly watching for the tight feeling in her chest and the self-righteous thoughts that put her at risk of lashing out at Jason. She knows these are Signs that her willpower tank is depleted. She understands the Habit Pathway that leads her in the wrong direction. Now when her body tightens, her awareness of the old Sign reminds her she's at a crossroads. Instead of charging toward the conflict, she exhales and leaves the room, Traveling in the right direction.

How can you set yourself up for success? Consider your resolution in terms of *where, what* and *when*.

In which specific location does your new activity happen? There might be multiple locations. For example, in addition to preparing her meals for home, Miranda has to work out how she will handle eating at restaurants, a friend's house, snacks on the road, etc. By preparing a specific plan for each setting, she is much more likely to stay on track. What settings do you need to plan for?

Next, consider if you have what you need where you need it. What items does your new behavior need to have handy? For example, if you intend to go to the gym after work, pack a bag of exercise clothes to take to work. Or if your new habit, like Marcus's, involves communication, having *what you need where you need it* means having the right words in mind when it's time for the challenging conversation. You might even prepare by writing out your thoughts so you have the right words ready when you need them.

What temptations need to be removed? Delete your social media apps if you want to stop absent-minded scrolling. Instead, load an interesting podcast onto your phone and put the podcast app in the spot where your social media icons used to be. Jasmin removed temptation by sitting on her hands during her slow breathing to prevent absent-mindedly chewing on her nails.

What emotional Signs need to be managed? In Exercise P4, you explored how HALT. Being Hungry, Angry, Lonely and Tired drains your willpower tank. What environmental cues can you set up to remind you to eat healthy, find calm, connect and restore your energy? Like Rachel, how can you pause when you feel depleted and take action to restore yourself?

What timing cues are needed? Decide when you will do your new action. Like Marcus picking this evening to talk with Kanesha, make a commitment to yourself for when you will take the first step.

Once you figure out *where, what* and *when* your new action will occur, *how* will you remember to do it if your autopilot takes over again? How can you use reminders or create physical Signs in your environment? Yolanda rearranged her kitchen to cue her commitment to healthier eating. What Signs will cue your new action?

Action-Able Exercise P16:
Set the stage for action

Collect your thoughts about what you've learned so far and prepare a customized action plan for your resolution. Engage your Manager to identify the key details.

Gather your staging notes:

What is my goal action? _____

_____

Where will my new action take place? _____

_____

What items or words do I need to have readily available?

_____

What temptations need to be removed? _____
_____

When will my new action happen?_____
_____

Declare your action plan by completing the following sentence:

I will prepare my environment by providing these items,
_____,

and removing these items, _____
_____.

I will prepare myself by having these words ready _____
_____.

I will do my new action in this location _____
at this time _____.

I will use these Signs to remind me of my new action:
_____.

Based on the action plan you laid out above, come up with multiple two-minute micro-actions you can take to set yourself up for success, such as setting a regular reminder in your phone, throwing away cigarettes or packing a lunch to take to work.

Make a list of micro-actions for your customized action plan.

The Preparation Phase of the habit life cycle is all about awareness and planning. The time you take to make a well-thought-out plan sets you up for success.[8] Now you know about your Hero, your community, your inner parts and your unique circumstances. You have prepared your mental, social and physical environment and set up timing cues. The characters and stage are set. You are ready for sustained action!

Chapter Recap

♦ Prepare the physical environment for success.

♦ Empower your Manager to remove items that activate your Tempted Self and to put needed objects where you will find them when it's time for your new behavior.

♦ We have a limited amount of willpower. Managing the environment helps conserve willpower for when it's really needed.

♦ When we live with other people, preparing the environment is usually more challenging. Let people know of your resolution and ask for a compromise.

♦ Prepare by collecting the right words to say in challenging situations.

- We often seek the "right moment" to do the hard thing, as if it will get easier later. Instead, identify a specific date and/or time for your new action.

- Think through when your new habit will fit into your regular routine. Think outside the box to create customized solutions that work for you.

- Prepare Signs to remind you to do your new habit.

- The trigger for the behavior you want to stop can be transformed into a cue for your resolution. This Sign indicates the crossroads between the old behavior and the new action and can offer an invitation to Travel in the new direction.

Key Words

When, Where, What (to remove or have available), How (to remember)

RESOLUTION PHASE
Action-Able Options

▶ Prepare your mental environment by exhaling and practicing KInDness, the keystone habit for persisting in the face of setbacks.

▶ Build compassion for yourself by thinking about how you would encourage a friend.

▶ Be inquisitive by focusing on the facts (who, what, when, where, how) with neutrality and curiosity.

▶ Strengthen your determination by focusing on the rewards of your resolution.

▶ Get to know all of the inner parts that support (KInD Coach, Manager and Future Self) and discourage (Inner Critic, Tempted Self and Saboteur) you.

▶ See each of these parts as if they are outside of you to become clearer about whose voice you hear in your mind as you work toward change.

▶ Prepare the inner social environment by strengthening the KInD Coach, Manager and Future Self. Use awareness to keep your attention on these supportive parts, especially when unsupportive inner parts are active.

▶ Prepare your outer social environment by fostering relationships with positive people in your life.

▶ Prepare your physical environment by removing temptations, providing needed supplies, preparing for each relevant location, deciding when the time is right and creating reminder Signs.

▶ Prepare a customized plan focused on your unique circumstances, tendencies, strengths and vulnerabilities.

Are any of these Action-Able steps relevant to this moment in your journey?

Download the relevant exercise worksheets at www.margithenderson.com/hope-to-habit-worksheets

PART III:

SUSTAINED ACTION PHASE

Persistence

*C*hange, the musical gets a bit boring in Act 4. The characters are doing the same scene over and over, but the music gets richer, as new harmonies and instrumental changes are layered in with each repetition. The real action is happening inside the Hero's brain.

Your brain is home to countless cells, called neurons, with long spidery arms that reach for the receiving arm of the next cell and use chemicals to communicate and connect with each other. When a thought or behavior happens over and over, neurons link up to create a neural network. As if dancing together in a conga line, "neurons that fire together wire together."[1] This biological process creates our autopilot experiences. We can do an action absent-mindedly because it's built into our brain and body memory.

Originally, brain scientists thought once a neural network was formed, it couldn't be changed. But modern imaging technology allows us to peer into the brain, and we've discovered how much action is really happening in there. Turns out when we do something new, the neurons let go and stretch in a different direction, reaching for other cells, changing the neural relationships in our brains. Referred to as neuroplasticity, a new action molds the brain, like plastic, into different forms. With enough repetition, these new neural networks hold their shape[2]

People often ask: How *long* does it take to form a new habit? As James Clear points out, "What people really should be asking is, 'How many does it take to form a new habit?' That is, how *many* repetitions are required to make a habit automatic?"[3] The answer is we must do our new action over and over and over and over and over. You get the idea. Sustained action creates a habit of our resolution by forming a new neural conga line in the brain.[4]

My bossy neural network has fired regularly over the past *five decades.* No wonder it's so difficult to mind my own business. I'm in a tough spot at this point—my brain is wired to do the thing I want to stop doing, but it hasn't yet developed the neural networks for my resolution. I notice many of my micromanaging comments before they cross my lips, and I cringe a bit when one slips through. I can be KInD with myself about this because I know I'm up against my biology and am working to reshape my brain. But even once I've mastered focusing on my own life rather than meddling, the old nosy network will still be there. *The neural network for an unrepeated action weakens; however, it cannot be eliminated.*

This is why the Preparation Phase is so important. By setting up our mental, social and physical environment for success, we remove Signs awakening the neural networks for the unwanted behavior and add Signs pointing toward the resolution.

All of the inner parts we met in the previous section are really just neural networks in action. Seeing them as characters in your internal show, rather than as brain cells, livens up the process and strengthens your awareness.

Early in the change process, the cellular connections for the disruptive inner parts might be stronger than those of your newly developing KInD Coach, Manager and Future Self. But we don't need to battle the Inner Critic, Tempted Self and Saboteur. We can accept these networks as inevitable given the brain science. Just meet these parts with awareness. The very act of *noticing* the disruptive part actually strengthens the neural pathway of the KInD Coach, who is the inquisitive observer.

During your Preparation Phase, you practiced a new dance move to pivot when you notice a disruptive inner part: Notice–Exhale–Redirect. Observe how your Tempted Self leers, while the Saboteur rationalizes to coax you off course. See how your Inner Critic condemns you for struggling. These parts are just doing their jobs. Notice them, exhale and redirect your awareness to the supportive people and inner parts. Your KInD Coach sees your misstep with compassion and helps the Hero regroup and go around the pitfall next time. The Manager prepares the environment to help you succeed, and the Future Self reminds you why it's all worth it.

Each Action-Able Exercise is designed to reshape your brain for change. By repeating the healthy new thoughts and behaviors over and over, we're building our Action-Able brain. While the Sustained Action Phase is the most difficult to get through, we have made it easier by preparing. We've set the stage for success, and we're ready to be KInD with ourselves as we persist in living our best intentions.

Chapter Recap

◆ When a thought or behavior happens over and over and over, brain cells link up to create a neural network.

◆ This biological process creates our autopilot experiences. We can do an action absent-mindedly because it's built into our brain and body memory.

◆ A new action molds the brain into different forms, and with enough repetition these neural networks hold their new shape. This is called neuroplasticity.

◆ The Preparation Phase sets up the mental, social and physical environment to stop activating the unwanted brain connection while sparking the neural networks for the resolution.

◆ The inner characters are just neural networks in action. Strengthen the supportive inner parts by meeting the disruptive parts with awareness. Notice the Inner Critic, Tempted Self and Saboteur, exhale and redirect your attention to the KInD Coach, Manager and Future Self.

◆ By repeating the healthy new thoughts and behaviors during the Sustained Action Phase, we're building our Action-Able brain.

◆ Each Action-Able Exercise is designed to reshape your brain for change.

Key Words

Neural Network, Neuroplasticity, Notice–Exhale–Redirect

Tracking Change

Tom hates pinching pennies and can't quite believe this is his life now. He and his wife, Carol, retired last year, finally arriving at the life of leisure and adventure they had spent decades working and saving for. But then the stock market crashed, wiping out the bulk of their retirement accounts. Now their monthly pension payments almost cover their essentials, but each month they struggle to deal with the gap. Tom's chest tightens as he worries about whether their remaining savings will be enough for their long-term needs. It wasn't supposed to be like this. Money had never been an issue for them before.

Learning to live on a tight budget is difficult under any circumstance. You might need to pay down debt, want to save up for a special purchase or be facing a job loss or savings hit like Tom and Carol experienced. Our financial wellbeing is the intersection of our life opportunities, which can be suppressed by external circumstances (such as discrimination or economic crises), and our personal and professional habits, over which we have the most control.

Tracking our spending is one of the most important financial habits we can develop. We often don't realize how money slips through our fingers until we pay close attention to what we buy.

Awareness is the linchpin for change. To build awareness about your resolution, consider how you will track your new action. Some things are easy to count, like Tom and Carol's dollars, Miranda's pounds, Jamal's minutes of concentration at work or even Jasmin's fingernail length. Other resolutions can't be counted. How do we track Rachel's calm, Marcus's reflective listening or my minding my own business? Somehow, we must find a way to assess our follow-through on the plan we made in Action-Able Exercise P16. By tracking our progress, we see our successes and discover where we have more to learn.

Here's the thing: We must be sure to assign the task of tracking change to the KInD Coach and the Manager. *In the hands of the Inner Critic, tracking can do more harm than good.* The Inner Critic watches our imperfect efforts to live our resolutions and finds ammunition to blast us with. Plus, the Saboteur looks for progress to rationalize a lapse.

Miranda is careful about tracking her weight because she knows her disruptive inner parts *weaponize* her focus on pounds. The Inner Critic jumps on her if her weight bumps up, and the Saboteur uses any weight loss to try to lead her astray. She sees how quickly they steer her thinking toward good versus bad. "If my weight goes down, I'm good. If my weight goes up, I'm bad." This leaves her looping between pride and shame.

Miranda reminds herself tracking is about KInD awareness and learning, not grading success or failure. She keeps the scale in her guestroom closet and weighs herself once a week. More important to Miranda is her recipe count. She tracks how many cooking experiments she has tried and enjoys watching the width of her recipe notebook grow.

Feeling proud of ourselves is an important motivator for change. However, when our pride is too linked to the goal, shame will always lurk nearby. Since setbacks happen throughout the Sustained Action Phase, we need to find a way out of this pride-shame loop.

The mind generally thinks in terms of good/bad, succeed/fail and right/wrong, so it's normal for this to occur. Just meet these thoughts with your new move: Notice–Exhale–Redirect to KInDness.

The secret to lasting change is to *anchor your pride to how you handle setbacks.* By focusing on learning from challenges, you take the sting out of reversals. When your mind says, "You're a failure because you just smoked that cigarette," your KInD Coach will notice the Inner Critic, accept this voice is just an old neural network talking, exhale and redirect you to being curious about the conditions setting you up to smoke this time. You discover a new stressor or Sign or thought pattern, and now you can strategize about how to prepare for it next time. Your KInD Coach celebrates you for handling the setback well.

Our KInD Coach is vigilant in detecting how the Saboteur tries to use success to urge you to lapse. This is how "pride comes before a fall."[1] The Saboteur uses our tracking success to woo us into giving in to temptation. Instead, we notice the rationalization and spot the Saboteur at work. Eventually we get better at seeing this process before we've lapsed, but we often miss it during the Sustained Action Phase, recognizing the Saboteur only in hindsight.

Tom is easily distracted from his frugal intentions. His eyes widen as he ventures into Costco for the first time. The Saboteur entices Tom to overspend by convincing him these bargains are too fabulous to pass up. Tom is excited to find such good prices on the upscale electronics he used to buy without a thought. When the cashier announces the total, Tom's stomach twists. He got carried away. Tom pays the bill, but as he walks out, he's making a mental list of the items he will return tomorrow.

The next time Tom shops at Costco, he keeps a running tally in his head so there are no surprises at the register. He dodges the temptations of the sample stations, considers the sale items carefully and skips the electronics department altogether. Tom is learning to make the choices his new circumstances demand.

Does your goal behavior lend itself to being counted? My exercise habit was boosted a few years ago when I got a watch with a fitness tracker. It gives me three circles I work to fill each day: general calories burned, number of minutes of vigorous exercise and standing hourly. I love watching the colorful coils expand over the course of the day. It bums me out when I realize in the middle of a walk I forgot to put on my watch. It almost seems like my exercise didn't happen if I don't measure it. I have to remind myself of this: My cardiovascular system still benefits even when my watch doesn't count the steps!

Pick a strategy for assessing your resolution action. Miranda and Yolanda use the Weight Watchers points system for tracking their food choices. The WW app makes it easy for them to find their food items and know where they stand with points for the day and week. The WW monitoring system doesn't prescribe dos and don'ts. Instead, it strengthens awareness and offers flexibility about food choices. Yolanda and Miranda learn and make adjustments.

You can also get creative with low-tech options for monitoring progress. For example, to track my weekly writing goal, I made a paperclip chain that hangs in my office to show my progress. I add a paperclip each time I write on a Sunday. Watching my progress accumulate reminds me not to break the chain.

Seeing progress—having visual trackers of your intended actions—keeps you focused on your resolution. Maybe your goal is to express thanks to your employees each day. You could put two small glasses on your desk and place 15 colorful beads in one glass. Over the course of the day, each time you offer appreciation, you move a bead from one glass to the other. The bright beads remind you of your resolution, and moving them lets you know if you've met your goal of expressing gratitude at least 15 times each day.[2]

Tracking change requires us to create a second habit. In addition to learning to eat healthier, Miranda and Yolanda also need to remember to use their tracking app on their phones. Watch for the Saboteur to attack this crucial solution, coaxing you to skip your monitoring process, to disrupt your awareness. Just notice the Saboteur, exhale and redirect back to tracking change.

What about habits that are hard to count? For my resolution to stop nagging, what do I track? The number of micro-managing thoughts that cross my mind? Or come out of my mouth? Even if I could bear to make those tally marks, it won't work in the flow of my day. Also, though we need the KInD Coach to watch for unhealthy behavior so we can understand what triggers it, it's more helpful to track the new behavior. When I mind my own business, what am I doing instead? These days, I'm thinking about and writing this book. A good indicator of my progress toward focusing on my own interests rather than meddling is tracking the word and page counts on this project.

Rachel has been working with a therapist for a month now and is writing in a journal to clear her thoughts. Her therapist asked Rachel to add a daily rating of her mood on a 0-to-10 scale, ranging from calm to agitated. Rachel sees how her slow exhalations and patience prayers keep her rating lower, calmer. Even touching her prayer bracelet reminds her to be KInD with herself and drops her rating a notch. Rachel's therapist teaches her that it's not realistic to always be calm, but the goal is to have lots of solutions to decrease the rating, moving from agitated to calm.

Jamal wishes his coworkers would stop interrupting him, that they would just know without his having to say anything. He's anxious about being more directly assertive, but he needs to find a way to concentrate so he can get his work done.

Jamal decides to do an experiment to boost his curiosity and willingness to try something new. He loves looking at data patterns—he's a geek like that. For a week, Jamal tracks his time on task without doing anything else differently. He already has a new block of uninterrupted time from 7a.m. to 10 a.m. During the second week, he shifts his lunch hour to eating before his teammates, and he logs another focused hour while his coworkers take their later lunch break. But when the group gets back to brainstorming, his teammates return to peppering him with questions and requests.

Jamal crafts an email explaining he does his best work during uninterrupted blocks of time. Rather than bombarding him throughout the day, he asks his coworkers to make a list of their ideas and proposes that he check in with them at 11 a.m., 1p.m. and 4 p.m. to talk through the next tasks they have for him. He holds his breath and clicks send, wondering if this will have any effect.

When we track our progress, we also catch our setbacks. Recently, I found myself wondering if my fitness tracking watch was broken. I was walking as usual, but my vigorous-exercise circle hardly moved two days in a row. I had walked for over an hour each day, and I was frustrated about not getting credit. But the data change sparked my curiosity. Instead of walking with my exercise buddy in person, we were talking on the phone while walking in different locations. I've always known I walk faster with her—she's a very speedy walker—but I didn't realize how much my pace slowed without her. The next day I did an experiment and stepped up my pace. My green circle filled right in. Turns out it was me, not my watch.

When you hit a setback, call on your KInD Coach to explore what happened. In my case, I discovered that when I walk alone I have to concentrate on walking faster than I naturally would. When you notice a change, be curious about what's helping or hindering your progress.

Create a tracking system for your goal. How will you count your steps? When you stick with the plan you made, your steps head in the direction of your Future Self. Steps backward are to be expected, but you want to catch them early and redirect. With tracking, you learn a new dance move to keep your forward momentum: Step–Back–Rock–Forward.

Yolanda didn't realize how many food choices she makes every day. Now that she's using the WW app, logging everything that goes in her mouth, she discovers how many mini snacks she noshes on throughout the day: a handful of chips here, a fistful of M&Ms there, here a soda, there some pretzels. It took only a few days of counting points to see the problem. Now Yolanda plans her daily snacks in the morning, when her willpower is strongest. Plus, having her own snack shelf makes it easier to stick with her plan.

Jamal is relieved that his team responds respectfully to his email. They designate a corner of their whiteboard for a Jam List, and his suggestion of specific check-in times seems to work. Jamal's tracking shows more time on task, and his coworkers see he can get their ideas implemented sooner this way. Win-win. Jamal is pleased his speaking up made a difference.

But old habits are hard to shake. Excited about their new ideas, his teammates can't resist getting his immediate input.

Step–Back–Rock–Forward. Jamal wonders what else might work. By week four, Jamal writes "can it wait?" on an orange Post-It note, taping it on his headphone facing the cubicle door. Twenty minutes later, he hears "hey, Jamal." He pretends not to hear and keeps working, wondering what will happen. Adam notices the note and remembers Jamal's request. "Oh, right," Adam says, turning to his team, "let's add that to our Jam List." Jamal's minutes on task keep ticking.

Throughout the day or at the end of each day, reflect on your progress and setbacks. Maybe you make time to journal, as Rachel does. Or, like Jamal, you keep a running tally and watch the experiment as it unfolds. Maybe you reflect while brushing your teeth before bed. You might put a Post-It note on your bathroom mirror saying "Reflect." Eventually, just seeing your face in the mirror will prompt you to review your day.

Action-Able Exercise SA1:
Track your change

- How will you count steps toward your Future Self?

- What did you learn from your observations of steps forward and back today?

- How does your action plan need to be modified to incorporate what you learned?

- What are you proud of about how you handled your change process today?

Use this reflection system to count your steps forward and back without judgment. Learn from your experience, confirming the parts of your plan that work and revising the plan where needed.

It's crucial that your daily reflection specifically reminds you to feel proud of yourself for your process. When you can find pride in how you handle a setback, then you've found the antidote to shame. By focusing on the process more than on the outcome, you become more resilient and Rock-Forward with an invigorated momentum.

Sustained action requires this combination of action, reflection and revision. We need to repeat the new behavior over and over until it is neurologically ingrained. We persist through challenges—stepping forward, stepping back, then rocking forward and moving ahead. Each step, whether forward or back, is an opportunity for learning, and for this we can feel proud.

Chapter Recap

- ◆ Awareness is the linchpin for change.

- ◆ Create a daily practice to track your steps forward and back as you work to embody your Future Self.

- ◆ Be sure to assign the task of tracking change to the KInD Coach and the Manager. The Inner Critic and

Saboteur can weaponize monitoring to activate shame or prompt a lapse.

◆ The mind generally thinks in terms of good/bad, succeed/fail and right/wrong. Notice–Exhale–Redirect to KInDness. Tracking is about KInD awareness and learning, not grading success or failure.

◆ The secret to lasting change is to anchor your pride to how you handle setbacks. By focusing on learning from challenges, you take the sting out of reversals.

Key Words

Awareness, Tracking, Step–Back–Rock–Forward, Reflect

The Reward Dilemma

Kanesha weeps with relief when the gastroenterologist tells them Marcus's tumor is benign. "Given your family history, you'll have to come back for regular checkups," she says, "but for now, you're fine." Marcus blinks. Having braced for the worst, he's not sure he heard the doctor right. Confused, he looks to Kanesha. She smiles through her tears. "You're OK, honey," she says, squeezing his hand.

In the days between the biopsy and getting these results, the floodgates had opened. Marcus talked to Kanesha more than he had during their prior 17 years of marriage. For the first time, Marcus told Kanesha about tending to his father during his long, complicated battle with cancer. None of the treatments helped. They just made his father's life miserable for years before he died. Marcus always knew he wouldn't consent to most types of cancer treatment for himself, if it ever came to that, but he'd never said anything to Kanesha. She was stunned to learn Marcus didn't want chemo or radiation if the tests showed cancer. "Nesha, I want to live with you as long as I possibly can," Marcus said earnestly, "but not like that. I can't do that to myself or you."

On the drive home from the doctor's office, relief washes over both of them. When he parks in front of their home,

Marcus turns to Kanesha. "I never imagined I could love you even more, but I do. Thank you, Nesha."

With each step Marcus takes to open up to his wife, he is rewarded with greater closeness and love. At first, he looked for her smile, and recently he sought Kanesha's understanding. The more Marcus speaks, the stronger their connection grows.

Rachel's slow breathing, prayer practice and journaling are changing how she feels in her body. She still gets tired, frustrated and agitated sometimes, but now she knows how to step away and get a grip. Rachel's new coping strategies are rewarded with calm.

Miranda can wear some of her old favorite outfits again and this feels great, but even more rewarding is the spaciousness of her mind. Since she's obsessing less about food she can't eat, Miranda has more mental room to think about the rest of her life.

But for Tom and Carol, their resolution doesn't feel rewarding yet. They're stuck in the Reward Dilemma, where the temptations to spend money are stronger than the rewards for sticking with their tight budget.

All habits, whether healthy or unhealthy, are driven by rewards.[1] Recall the Habit Pathway: Signs —> Fuel —> Travel —> Destination. The Destination is the reward, and it motivates (Fuels) us to do an action (Travel). When we're trying to Travel in a new direction, *toward* our resolution and *away from* the absent-minded, obsessive or avoidant behavior, we find ourselves at a crossroads. During the Sustained Action Phase, the reward for the unwanted action is still very enticing, but the rewards of the new action might not be strong enough yet to get us moving in the right direction. No wonder it can be so hard to change!

To consistently live our best intentions, we must better understand how rewards work.

Rewards can be physical, social, sensory and/or emotional. A physical reward is an enjoyable thing we get after an action, like Jasmin's fun fingernail appliqués or the raises Tom used to get at work. Social rewards are the positive attention we get from other people, such as Kanesha smiling at Marcus or Sergio complimenting the tasty dinner Miranda has made. I get a yummy sensory reward from eating chips, but I can get a similar salty, crunchy sensation by eating nuts. Emotional rewards are embedded in all of these reinforcements, because they make us happier.

Emotional rewards are extra powerful because they're biological and immediate. As we explored before, dopamine fuels craving, powerfully motivating our choices. Change experts sometimes talk about "dopaminizing" a new habit to make it emotionally irresistible.[2]

These strategies try to trick the Tempted Self into wanting the healthy behavior by linking it with a thrilling experience. But this approach might not work because many of the actions we struggle to do are hard to pair with a dopamine spike, yet most of the unhealthy habits we're trying to stop have intense, immediate dopamine rewards, making them difficult to resist. This vexing situation amplifies the Reward Dilemma.

If you can't find a way to *dopaminize* your resolution, look for ways to boost oxytocin, a hormone that calms the body through relationship.[3] For example, I *oxytocinize* my exercise routine by doing it with my friend. Our connection is a compelling social-emotional reward for my workout routine.

Often overlooked, relief might be the most powerful emotional reward of all. In fact, you can break rewards into two types: positive reinforcements and relief experiences.

All of the reward examples we've talked about so far are pleasant rewards. Something positive is added after an action, making us want to do this behavior again.

In contrast, a relief reward is when a painful experience *stops* after the behavior.* When you're miserable beforehand and you do something that makes your agony stop, it gets your attention and your brain maps a path back to that action. Going for a run after a stressful workday releases physical tension and frustration, creating a relief reward. On the other hand, road rage is also rewarded by tension relief.

The Saboteur uses relief about our progress to tempt us to lapse. The Halo Effect happens when the Saboteur encourages us to order a Diet Coke to relieve stress about weight loss (relief reward) and then tempts us to order french fries,

---

* The technical term for relief rewards is negative reinforcement, which is often confused with punishment. Punishment is when a behavior is followed by the *addition* of a painful experience, whereas negative reinforcement is when an action causes the pre-existing painful experience to *cease*. With negative reinforcement (relief rewards), the pain happens before the behavior, not after, as in punishment, and it stops after the behavior.

which is pleasantly rewarded with a yummy taste. Double points for the Saboteur.

Tom is accustomed to getting pleasant rewards. He got bonuses at work when he hit sales goals. He and Carol celebrated anniversaries and birthdays with generous gifts and fancy dinners out. Now their new frugal behaviors are encouraged with relief rewards. Tom's anxiety about having overspent was calmed the next morning when he went back to Costco and returned the electronics that blew the budget. He's stressed about their money running out, and this angst decreases (relief reward) when he sticks to his budget.

Habits are often reinforced by both pleasant rewards and relief rewards. For example, smoking a cigarette generally calms a smoker (pleasant reward). But there's also a relief reward, because smokers usually experience a subtle physical tension and anxious agitation before lighting up. The act of smoking stops these unpleasant sensations (relief reward).

Remember the relief reward *subtracts* and the pleasant reward *adds*. It might be two sides of the same coin—subtract anxiety, add calm. The desire to remove anxiety is generally a stronger motivator for smoking because the act of not smoking leaves the person stuck with those unpleasant feelings. The same dynamics are at play when people struggle with emotional eating or spending.

Rachel's therapist helps her see how raging at Jason is rewarded by relief. When her body churns with agitation, triggered by helpless frustration from work or traffic or Jason not doing his chores, Rachel feels so edgy that she can hardly hold it in. When the dam bursts and she unleashes her fury on Jason, the roiling energy pours out. The tension of trying to hold back this torrent is immediately relieved, and her body feels calmer. But later the grief and guilt hit and her stomach sinks. Rachel sees how rage takes her from agitation to relief, but then to shame. Her new coping strategies empower her to go from anger to calm, without the shame, but it's more challenging to do in the moment.

I can relate to Rachel. When catastrophic fears squeeze my heart, I can hardly bear the tension in my body urging me to check, remind, suggest, meddle and nag. As soon as I intervene, my body relaxes and I feel reassured—this time I've averted the imagined disaster. But when I don't say anything, my anxiety surges. "Has he taken his medicine?" "Is it safe for her to drive so far?" I'm left to tolerate my heart in the vise grip of anxiety. Redirecting myself is difficult. The quick relief of reminding him "don't forget to take your medicine" is so much easier on me than trying to muzzle myself, calm my body and distract my mind. But the voice of my Future Self calls me forward, reminding me that my children need me to step back so they can find their own way.

To break the power of relief rewards that steer us in the wrong direction, we need to develop healthy relief rewards to insert into our Habit Pathway.

It's always helpful to start with an exhalation. Your slow breathing practice is the keystone habit that opens the door for other relief rewards. This will improve your ability to pause and plan, empowering you to choose other actions to create lasting relief so you live your best intentions and prevent the Shame Loop.

The Saboteur might try to disrupt your use of healthy relief rewards by casting doubt. "Slow breathing is silly. It can't possibly make you feel as good as this temptation. You can't get through the pain of feeling lonely, inadequate, upset without the comfort of the old behavior." Your Tempted Self will churn the edgy feeling in your body to try to make you buckle. Sometimes they will succeed at coaxing you back to your old habits so the painful feeling goes away more quickly. But your KInD Coach will be there with compassion and determination to help you back to the resolution road. The Future Self reminds you that the way to true relief is to make the healthy choice so you can feel relief *and* pride in your change process.

Play with your breathing by trying the following variations.[4] Take a moment now to exhale all the way out, making an *Ssssss* sound like a balloon releasing all of its air, then inhale with ease. On your next exhalation, make a gentle *Shhhhh* sound as you exhale all the way. For your second *Shhhhh* exhalation, place your hand on your heart and imagine patting the back of a sleepy baby resting on your shoulder. Allow your stress to feel comforted by this affection, *Shhhhh* . Then inhale with ease.

Notice your throat, chest and belly as you do this sequence again. *Sssss*, then inhale, *Shhhhh*, inhale. How do these sounds feel different in your body? Now try an *Ahhhhh*—the sound of relief. How are the body sensations of this sound different yet again? Where do you feel each exhalation? *Sssss, Shhhh, Ahhhh.* Feel the calm and relief of stress, anxiety, agitation and anger that come with even one cycle of this breathing pattern. Doing this routine for 30 seconds is a powerful relief solution.

Find new reward options by exploring enjoyable and soothing experiences that tap into each of your senses: sight, sound, smell, taste, touch and movement. What are your favorite activities to relax your body and mind? For example, you might enjoy:

- Watching the Nature Channel (sight)
- Listening to music (sound)
- Going for a walk (movement, sight)
- Having a cup of coffee or tea (taste, smell, touch)
- Playing an instrument (sound, touch)
- Petting your dog (touch, smell, sight)
- Working in your garden (sight, smell, touch, movement)
- Cooking (smell, taste, sight, sounds, touch)

Look for activities that leave you feeling calm or refreshed.

Tom finds retirement more rewarding now that he and Carol have taken up bird watching. Bundled up on a brisk winter walk a few months back, they came upon several neighbors standing on the road, all shading their eyes and staring up at the sky. A falcon was riding the current above them. Intrigued by this magnificent raptor, Tom and Carol got curious about what other birds they might find in their region.

On this spring day, Tom and Carol are taking a day trip, snaking along Maine's winding coastal roads toward Acadia National Park. They're excited to put their Lifetime Senior Pass to use for the first time. Not the African safari they dreamt about before retirement, but a rewarding nature treasure hunt nonetheless. Carol reads through the list of birds they're seeking: 21 nesting warbler species, not to mention the Atlantic puffin and bald eagle.

Action-Able Exercise SA2:
Develop healthy relief rewards

Create a feast for your senses. List healthy ways to activate relief rewards below and check the boxes for the senses impacted by each enjoyable activity.

Enjoyable Experiences	sight	sounds	taste	smell	sensation
slow exhalations (*Ssss, Shhh, Ahhh*)		X			X

How will you remember to do your calming sensory activities when you need relief?

Create reminders (Signs) of your options for soothing. You could create a series of index cards with words or an image on each card to remind you of ways to create relief rewards and keep these cards in your bag or at your desk. Or make a list on your phone.

Play with all types of rewards: physical, social, sensory and emotional rewards that add a pleasant experience and/or offer relief. These Destinations will Fuel your journey through the Sustained Action Phase.

Understanding What Fuels You

Rachel knows to watch like a hawk for the edginess that puts her at risk of blowing up. She must catch the tension early before it's overwhelming (Fuel). That's when slowing her breathing has the best chance to work and she can turn the other direction at this crossroads. Physically removing herself from the situation, she Travels toward her resolution. Once she's in the other room, Rachel quickly unwinds the mala beads and says her prayer. Sometimes she paces back and forth to release some of the energy coursing through her veins (de-Fuel). Raging feels like emotional vomiting. When your stomach's been churning with bile, you feel relieved after you throw up. Raging at Jason is like emotionally puking on him, leaving a relationship cleanup for afterward. When Rachel makes it to her journal in time, she hurls the rage onto the pages and contains it so no one gets hurt. It takes longer for her body and mind to calm down this way (longer and more complicated Travel), but when she's breathing, praying and journaling to get from agitated to calm, there's real relief, followed by pride (True Destination) instead of shame. Hard to do, but so worth it—a compelling relief reward.

Consider the behavior you'd like to change. How are rewards at play? For example, the real problem causing procrastination usually isn't time management or prioritizing our tasks. Procrastination is driven by relief rewards. When we start thinking about the dreaded task, we feel stressed, insecure, overwhelmed or discouraged and the Inner Critic goes after us. The angst and negative self-talk are relieved when we push them all away, assigning the task to our Future Self.[5] Procrastination has powerful relief rewards in the moment, even if we enter the Shame Loop later. But when we develop the emotional skills to break through procrastination and complete the project we've been avoiding, the relief about getting it done feels amazing. Plus, then we get a bonus pleasant reward—feeling proud of ourselves.

Like Rachel, we need to find new ways to handle the uncomfortable feelings we're avoiding and succeed in creating lasting change. When you translate *Don't* into *I will*, the most successful substitute behaviors will address the underlying tensions and painful feelings. Instead of having a stiff drink at the end of a stressful day, seeking to numb frustration (relief reward), make a plan to go for a brisk walk with a supportive friend to release the tension in your body and feel connected.

All relaxation activities harness relief rewards (removing tension or loneliness) and pleasant rewards (adding calm or connection).

What are the unpleasant emotions or body sensations happening before your obsessive, absent-minded or avoidant behavior? Remember the Fuel for an absent-minded behavior will be really subtle, while the Fuel for obsessive behaviors is intense, even if we don't always recognize it. Watch for the feelings you want to make stop or avoid altogether, such as anxiety, agitation, sadness, helplessness, loneliness or insecurity.

To discover how emotional rewards Fuel your behavior, invite your inquisitive KInD Coach to observe your emotional life. For example, can you tell the difference between feeling excited and content? Between feeling anxious and angry? Notice what different emotions are like in your body and mind.

As your emotional awareness increases, you will discover that emotions are made up of thoughts and body sensations. Your body probably feels energetic when you're excited and calm when you're contented. But anxious and angry have amped-up body sensations, too, so how do we tell the difference between excited, anxious and angry? The thoughts going through your mind will show you which emotion you are feeling. When we're energized with excitement, we think about something we're looking forward to. When our body feels an edgy energy and our thoughts are filled with worries about the future, we're afraid. But if the edgy energy is paired with thoughts of how we've been wronged, we might be angry rather than anxious. To improve your emotional awareness, check out the feeling and body sensation words listed in Appendix A. What thoughts and sensations go with the feelings you want to experience? What about for the emotions you want to avoid?

The Reward Dilemma is that our unhealthy habit offers a known shortcut to relief, while our new healthy action often involves Travel on a longer, unfamiliar path to a positive Destination. The old habit is just easier to do when we feel unsettled.

Today, Jamal can't bring himself to hold his boundary when his coworkers slide back into their old habit of interrupting him. He knows they're stressed by the project deadline, and he's worried they'll get mad at him if he reminds them to wait until he's ready for a break. But Jamal knows he's adding to the problem by being overly accommodating. He tries to muster the courage to tell them what he needs. After all, he's crunching for the same deadline. But his gut twists with nervousness about pissing them off. Jamal decides to just deal with their interruptions today. Avoiding conflict with his coworkers, his body relaxes. His old unwanted avoidant behavior is reinforced with a relief reward.

Jamal calms himself by avoiding conflict, but I don't. I head right into conflict when I'm stressed, pestering my kids about my latest concern. Like Rachel, I need a substitute behavior that offers relief.

What can I do instead of micromanage? Charles Duhigg points out, "You can't extinguish a bad habit, you can only change it."[6] He emphasizes that the best way to transform an unwanted habit is to substitute a new behavior *offering the same reward*. What substitute action can I do that will lead to the same reward? Mapping my Habit Pathway helps me think through what to do instead.

Here is my existing Habit Pathway where I calm myself by micromanaging: Kid Worry (Sign) —> Anxiety (Fuel) —> Micromanage (Travel) —> Anxiety Relief (Destination). I need to handle the anxiety Fueling my micromanaging differently to find a better path to relief.

I've tried turning my attention away from my kids and onto my own life and interests, but this requires that I ignore them, and that doesn't feel right or offer relief. After lots of trial and error, I discovered I can *oxytocinize* my new habit.

I'm lucky to have sweet relationships with each of my children. They are open-hearted, passionate and caring people, and we mostly enjoy each other's company. While I can gin up lots of worries about the future, in the present moment, my kids are safe and sound and our family is warmly connected. Instead of reaching for them with anxiety, I can savor our family's connection as my substitute behavior. Thinking about my loving relationship with each of them calms me.

Now when I notice a worry about my kids, I exhale, orient to love and redirect to focus on gratitude for my connection with them, reminding myself of how capable they are. The relief I feel helps me to lovingly let them go on with their own lives. My Lovingly-Let-Go Habit Pathway is: Kid Worry (Sign) —> Love (Fuel) —> Think about Connection (Travel) —> Anxiety Relief (Destination).

The Sign and Destination are the same in my new Habit Pathway. I've just fiddled with the middle parts. *I don't need to resist the craving for relief. I just take a different route to get there.* Plus, when I take my resolution road, I get bonus pleasant rewards of feeling proud of myself and my kids.

Mapping the Reward Dilemma

The crossroads intersecting at the healthy habit you're developing (resolution road) and the behavior you want to stop (detour) can be best understood by imagining diverging Habit Pathways.

Now when I notice feeling worried about my kids, I pause at the intersection. Which way will I turn? My old habit is to calm myself by checking or nagging. My resolution is to calm myself by focusing on love and connection.

Unfortunately, my micromanaging habit is a neural superhighway in my brain because that action has been taken countless times, while the new path is a new road just now being paved by my sustained action. It's still very easy to hop on the highway to get to calm sooner and more easily. But the highway also leads to disappointment and disconnection with my children, so it's really the detour. The path being paved is my resolution road.

To make sure we take the turn to our True Destination, we need to add clear Signs so we don't miss the turn.

Let's map out Jamal's Reward Dilemma to show you what I mean.

Jamal's lack of assertiveness at work has an avoidant dynamic. The Habit Pathway for Jamal's unwanted action is:

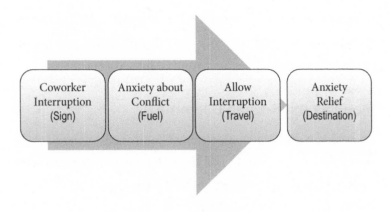

Jamal's Detour Habit Pathway

Jamal's overly accommodating behavior is rewarded by anxiety relief but, because he's not getting his work done, Jamal also ends up frustrated and resentful. His work anxiety builds when he avoids conflict with his coworkers, and he feels overwhelmed and ineffective. Since applying the Action-Ability Approach to his situation, Jamal creates the time blocks he needs so he can concentrate better at work.

Let's map out the Habit Pathway for Jamal's resolution road. Sometimes it works best to think through the pathway out of order.

Start with Travel (the habit being developed): Jamal claims uninterrupted time by using early morning hours, taking an early lunch and holding to scheduled check-ins with his team. Next, the True Destination of the resolution road: Jamal enjoys the flow he can get into when uninterrupted, the feeling of accomplishment from completing his tasks and the relief of his work anxiety. Now that he sees what's possible when he defends the time blocks he needs, his craving for uninterrupted time is even stronger. This desire Fuels his willingness to get to work before his coworkers arrive and to speak up when they forget and interrupt him.

Jamal creates Signs to remind himself how much he enjoys the work flow he experiences when he claims the time he needs to focus. He finds a photo online of a kayaker effectively maneuvering through rapids, with the current propelling him forward. The picture reminds him of how he feels when he's on a roll with his work. He prints a copy of this picture and tacks it up in his cubicle just below the spot where his coworkers tend to pop their heads over the wall to ask a question. When he looks at an interrupting coworker, he also sees his Sign. The photo Fuels Jamal by activating his longing for focus and makes him willing to do the Travel of reminding his teammate that he'd rather wait until it's time to review the Jam List.

To strengthen his reminder even more, Jamal makes a Sign to remind him of the negative outcomes when he allows interruptions. He finds a photo of a barge slowly moving through a canal's lock system. He photoshops a kayaker image next to the barge, showing the kayaker trapped in the lock system, itching to get off the canal and back onto the rapids.

Both of Jamal's kayaker images Fuel his craving for the feeling of accomplishment he experiences when he defends his time blocks.

Think of it this way: The Habit Pathway for the resolution road has three types of Signs to make sure we avoid the detour.

The first is the Stop Sign, which is the trigger for the un-wanted habit (in Jamal's case, a coworker interruption). The

Stop Sign reminds us to pause at the intersection to decide which direction we will Travel.

The second is the Detour Alert, which reminds us that the usual action, even if initially rewarding, ultimately takes us somewhere we don't want to go. Jamal's picture of the kayaker stuck on the canal reminds him of how frustrated he feels when he allows interruptions.

Third, the Turn Signal points to the resolution road. Jamal's picture of the kayaker propelled forward stirs the feeling of excitement (Fuel) to make the Turn and Travel to his True Destination.

Now we have all the parts of Jamal's Habit Pathway to his resolution road:

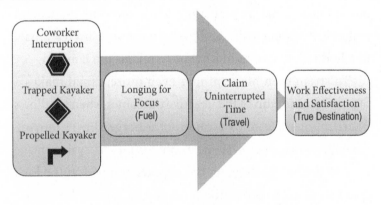

Jamal's Resolution Road Habit Pathway

When Jamal hits the Stop Sign (coworker interruption), he could go either way. But his Detour Alert and Turn Signal (kayaker images) remind him that he's at the crossroads. He realizes that he must deal with anxiety either way. If he relieves his stress by avoiding the conflict and allowing the interruption, he ends up overwhelmed and anxious about work. When he defends his time blocks to lessen his work angst, he has to face his anxiety about pushing back on his teammates. Because both roads go through anxiety, Jamal sees that he can't avoid some version of stress but realizes that the more rewarding situation happens when he claims his time. This motivates him to speak up.

Note that we've been practicing a turning point keystone habit for several chapters now: Notice–Exhale–Redirect. We see the trigger for the old habit, the Stop Sign. Our exhalation is our keystone Turn Signal. Exhaling calms the body and mind, which de-Fuels the urge for the detour and re-Fuels us to turn onto the resolution Habit Pathway.

By mapping out the Reward Dilemma, we see how to get to the True Destination instead of returning to the detour. We spot the crossroads and make the turn.

Action-Able Exercise SA3:
Your Reward Dilemma Map

Map out your diverging Habit Pathways by filling in the boxes below.

First, start with your Detour Habit Pathway: the absent-minded, obsessive or avoidant habit you want to change. In the Travel box, write down the unwanted action. Then, in the Destination box, note all of the pleasant and relief rewards that draw you back to this old habit. Next, identify what emotions Fuel you, propelling you toward the detour behavior. These are the uncomfortable feelings that set up a relief reward or the enticing feelings from pleasant rewards. Finally, figure out what Signs point you to the unwanted action and write them in the first box.

Your Detour Habit Pathway

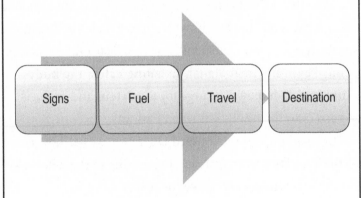

Next, map out the details of your Resolution Habit Pathway. First, fill in the Travel box: What is the new habit you're working on? In the Destination box, write in all of the pleasant and relief rewards you can think of for your resolution action. Include physical, social, sensory and emotional rewards. Now back it up and identify the Fuel. What are the emotions of longing, anticipation, excitement and hope that energize you to take your habit action (Travel) to get these rewards?

Now let's figure out your Signs. The Stop Sign is easy because it's the same as the Sign you identified above at the start of your Detour Habit Pathway. Next, consider your Detour Alert: What are the negative outcomes of your detour habit? The final step is to figure out your Turn Signal. In addition to an exhalation, what cues will prompt you to turn here and Travel to your True Destination? These three Signs remind you to pause and turn at the intersection and Fuel you to skip the detour and Travel to your True Destination.

Your Resolution Habit Pathway

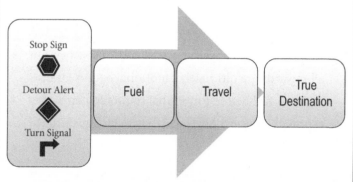

Consider these maps a work in progress. Update them as you gain new insights.

The Sustained Action Phase is a period of learning through trial and error. When you hit a setback, be inquisitive about the cues, cravings and rewards that made you take the detour. Call on your determination to use these insights to further illuminate your resolution Habit Pathways and Reward Dilemma.

Chapter Recap

- All habits, whether healthy or unhealthy, are Fueled by rewards.

- During the Sustained Action Phase, there is a Reward Dilemma. The reward for the unwanted action is still very enticing, calling us in the wrong direction, and the rewards of the new action might not be strong enough yet to excite us about Traveling toward our resolution.

- Rewards can be physical, social and/or sensory, but all rewards are ultimately emotional because they make us feel better. Emotional reinforcements are especially powerful because they're biological and immediate.

- Rewards come in two types: pleasant rewards and relief rewards. Pleasant rewards add a positive experience after the action. With relief rewards, an unpleasant experience stops when we do the action.

- Look for other ways to create relief, such as exhaling slowly (your keystone habit). All relaxation activities harness relief rewards (removing tension) and pleasant rewards (adding calm). Enjoy calming activities that activate your senses (sight, sound, smell, taste, touch, movement).

◆ The crossroads between the healthy habit you're developing (resolution road) and the behavior you want to stop (detour) can be best understood by imagining diverging Habit Pathways.

◆ The Resolution Habit Pathway includes three Signs. The Stop Sign is the trigger of the detour habit. The Detour Alert highlights the negative outcomes of the detour habit. The Turn Signal orients us to the rewards of the True Destination and Fuels us with excitement, motivating us to Travel to our resolution.

Key Words

Reward Dilemma, Pleasant Rewards, Relief Rewards, Resolution Habit Pathway, Stop Sign, Detour Alert, Turn Signal

15

Willpower and Stillpower

Yolanda feels as if she's a bartender trying to stay sober. The electric mixer pulses as she mashes the buttery potatoes for Roger and the kids, while she sautés riced cauliflower for herself. The Tempted Self eyes the potatoes, as the Saboteur whispers, "Just a little taste to make sure it has enough salt." Yolanda's made this recipe countless times and knows the potatoes are fine. She turns her attention to her dish. The olive oil, garlic and salt will make the cauliflower tasty, too. Night after night, Yolanda makes her WW recipes, plus an extra yummy side dish for her family to keep them content while they eat her WW main dish. But she's not sure how much longer she can keep this up.

We know willpower is a limited resource. When we ask too much of ourselves, our willpower tank gets depleted. But to develop our new habit, we need to maintain our willingness to get through the Sustained Action Phase. This is the most challenging part of our journey.

Each component of the Action-Ability Approach is designed to strengthen your willingness. By clarifying and simplifying your resolutions and preparing your environment, AAA helps you generate and conserve willpower for when you really need it.

We need willingness to chug up the hills. The two big hills are when we need to (1) use willpower to act on our resolution even when we don't want to and (2) use stillpower to avoid an unhealthy habit even when we have a strong urge to do it.[1]

As adults, each day, we all do the unpleasant jobs required to make our lives function: We do dishes, we pay bills, we get up early to go to work, we make cold calls, we pick up dog poop, etc. There are lots of chores that aren't particularly rewarding but must be done, and somehow we do them. How do we mobilize to overcome avoidance of these unpleasant or boring tasks?

We need to draw on this strength during the Sustained Action Phase, because the biology works against us. Our new brain pathways are still under construction. Our repetition builds the neural networks for the thoughts, feelings and urges that eventually support our new healthy habit, but the existing neural networks are a superhighway that pulls us off course.

A hallmark of the Sustained Action Phase is that we often don't want to do our resolution. We need willingness to propel us forward.

One of the biggest obstacles to lasting change is the belief that we can perfectly design our Habit Pathway so we always want to do the resolution. While we can improve our willingness by making the pathway more rewarding, the Reward Dilemma means we sometimes won't want to do our resolution. Fortunately, our progress doesn't need to be held hostage by our wants—we can find willingness to persist, even when we don't want to.

When your willpower tank is low, call AAA (your Action-Ability Approach) for re-Fueling.

Your Future Self can remind you why your resolution matters. Your Manager can find a two-minute micro-resolution to jump-start your engagement. Your KInD Coach is there to encourage you.

What gives you the boost you need to get up the hill?

Yolanda refills her tank by calling Miranda while she's cooking. Tonight, it's shrimp and cheesy grits for her family, and Yolanda is whisking up a tasty dressing for the salad she's having with her shrimp. Yolanda wants to dig into the grits, but even more so, she wants to continue wearing the cute new top she just bought. Yolanda knows she can find the willingness to eat her salad even when her tongue is craving grits.

Ultimately, thoughts are just thoughts, feelings are just feelings, and they can differ from your body's actions. Draw on willpower to live your best intentions even when your thoughts and emotions point elsewhere. You can order a soda instead of a beer even if your mind is preoccupied with a craving for alcohol. You can still write the report for work even though it's boring and you really don't want to.

When you feel stuck, come back to a micro-resolution. For example, I reorient to a two-minute writing goal when my mind feels frozen. Sometimes all I get out is a few sentences. That's fine. At least I've pushed ahead, showing myself I could write something even when my mind tells me I can't or it won't be good enough.

During the Sustained Action Phase, the Saboteur whispers in your ear, "Give up. This is too hard." The Tempted Self says, "Don't bother. It's not worth it." And the Inner Critic is sure you can't do it anyway.

You might be concerned your resolution is threatened by the presence of conflicting thoughts and feelings. You might believe you need to banish these unsupportive inner characters before you can succeed in your behavior change. But this isn't true.

When you hit the crossroads, you see the Stop Sign, Detour Alert and Turn Signal pointing you to your resolution. But the Inner Critic, Saboteur and Tempted Self might be in the backseat of your car, filling your mind with disruptive thoughts and your body with unpleasant feelings.[2] Your job is to Notice-Exhale-Redirect. Your KInD Coach is in the passenger seat. You're the driver. Turn the steering wheel in the direction of your resolution road, even as the ruckus from the backseat persists.

Fighting with unpleasant emotions keeps you tangled up in your pain. Similarly, when you try to push away negative thoughts, you're still focused on those thoughts. You can allow your conflicting thoughts, feelings and urges to be there, recognizing them as your biology in action. Act the way you want to feel. Notice the conflicting inner experience, exhale and redirect to the next two-minute action that keeps you on course.

Rachel's Turn Signal is a bright green sticky note on the cover of her journal that prompts her to "Be Nana, not Dad."

But tonight, Rachel is tired and itching for a fight. The Tempted Self feeds her a narrative to justify her urge to yell at Jason. Rachel knows she needs to step back—literally. Even though her thoughts and feelings are pushing her toward Jason, Rachel's KInD Coach reminds her that her agitation isn't about him. She turns her body and walks out of the room. Rachel gets to her bedroom, picks up her journal and just holds it, staring at the green note. *Shhhhh*, she exhales. "Don't be Dad," she reminds herself. "Be Nana."

It takes only two seconds for Rachel to pivot her body and move away, but this simple motion is challenging to do with so much inner pressure pushing her toward a fight. It takes more than two minutes to calm herself. But she can do it.

Tom has an easier time of it. Unlike Rachel or Yolanda, who have obsessive behaviors to contend with, Tom's detour habit involves absent-minded behaviors. His thoughts point him toward extravagance out of habit, but as soon as he remembers his new situation, he can redirect himself fairly easily. Tom's Future Self taps him on the shoulder and reminds him to keep a running tally at the store. Or to cancel the online order he's just purchased with an absent-minded "Buy Now" click. After emptying his virtual shopping cart, he protects himself for the future by finding his settings and deleting his "one-click" purchase option.

Tom still mourns the retirement he expected. He wishes they could travel and go out to fancy dinners, but even more he wants to protect the remaining savings for their long-term needs. Bird watching helps Tom discover that he can find the spirit of their dream adventures closer to home. Taking this idea further, he and Carol decide to mimic the international experiences they'd expected in retirement by exploring in their own kitchen. They find online videos showing them how to cook Vietnamese noodle bowls, Moroccan chicken tagine, Mexican mole sauce, African jollof rice. They order the needed spices online, and the rich smells transport them to faraway places.

Tom works with pleasant rewards to become willing to create a retired life different from the one he imagined. Rachel focuses on the Turn Signal that points her to the micro-resolution of stepping away. Yolanda asks for support to replenish her willpower tank. I use the social reward of visiting with my friend to get myself to go to the gym. What helps you find the energy to take your next step up the hill?

Action-Able Exercise SA4:
Strengthen your willpower

Do a task you don't want to do. Keep it short, less than five minutes, and set a timer. For example, you might respond to an email you've been avoiding or sweep up the mouse poop in your garage or read an opinion piece written by someone you disagree with politically.

Practice awareness of your discomfort and willingness while you stick with the task until the five-minute timer goes off.

Since you could do this arbitrary action, you can find willingness to do a two-minute action for your resolution even when you don't want to. Re-Fuel yourself with self-care or support first. Focus on your commitment to your Future Self and the reasons your goal matters.

Take notes about these experiences and how you activated your willpower and determination to act.

You can get yourself to do the thing you don't want to do, but be KInD with yourself about these uphill treks. We have only so much stamina for pushing ourselves forward. This needs to happen only occasionally.

I am reminded again of our family's hike through the Costa Rican rainforest. The rustling leaves, squawking birds and howling monkeys amped up my fear as dusk descended. I wanted to run even before encountering the viper, but I was willing to slow down and tolerate my anxiety because I wasn't going to leave my father. I could override my urge to dash for the exit. I controlled my feet even though I couldn't control my imagination or my fears. I used willpower—I will stay with my father—and stillpower—I won't run. Focusing on the connection with my family helped me manage my behavior in the moment, but the experience inside of me was as wild as the jungle I was walking through.

——— • ———

You'll know you've reached the Habit Phase when you regularly *want* to do your new action. Until then, expect inner protest. This is normal.

Your key Action-Able solution is to Notice–Exhale–Redirect. This is not to be confused with a "just think positive" pep talk. Telling yourself to think positively sets up a should rule, creating an inner power struggle. Instead, see these thoughts, feelings and urges for what they are, remnants of your current brain pathways.

Alcoholics Anonymous is "the largest, most well-known and successful habit-changing organization in the world," describes Charles Duhigg.[3] Using a 12-step program, AA helps alcoholics learn that, while the craving for alcohol may always be there, addicts can still find ways to stay sober. Alcoholics learn they can withstand the surge of temptation until it passes, while taking action to connect.

Emotions and urges can feel overwhelming, but when we don't act on them, they eventually subside. You can watch your unpleasant inner experience rise up like a wave. Keep watching and you will see that the emotional wave ultimately crests and falls. Referred to as Urge Surfing, you can observe without action while feelings peak and then release.[4]

My substitute behavior when I have the urge to nag is to manage my mouth while coping with my anxiety. My thoughts won't leap out of my mouth unless I move my lips. I can want to say something but instead use my stillpower to be quiet. It's a work in progress, but I'm much better than I was before we started this journey together.

Action-Able Exercise SA5:
Strengthen your stillpower

Explore the experience of sitting still for two minutes. Find a comfortable position, set an alarm for two minutes, close your eyes and sit.

If you have an itch, allow it without scratching. Direct your awareness to the pinky toe of your left foot (unless this is where the itch is, in which case, attend to your right foot). If your phone rings, let it ring without answering. The caller can leave a message. If you feel fidgety, notice the energy within you that wants to move and nonetheless remain still. Watch your inner experience as you would watch clouds move across the sky. Or maybe you imagine each experience just bubble up and then disappear. Observe your enjoyment or discomfort during this exercise. Just watch. Allow whatever comes up without action.

Take notes about your experience during this exercise. How did you allow conflicting thoughts, feelings and urges while you controlled your body's movement?

This exercise is about resisting, yet it's described in positive terms. Rather than saying "don't move," it says "stay still." Instead of "don't scratch the itch," it says "allow the itch and redirect your attention to a non-itchy part of your body." Rather than "don't answer the phone," the instruction is allow the phone to ring and go to voicemail. The directions tell you what to *do* rather than giving you a list of *don'ts*. The goal is to watch the urge to move as it rises and falls.

The breakthrough of the Action-Ability Approach occurs when we discover we can choose our resolution even while our inner howler monkeys are carrying on inside. Just notice those inner experiences—they're to be expected—and then exhale and redirect to doing your resolution anyway. With repetition during the Sustained Action Phase, the inner experience eventually aligns with the new action. Then you know you've reached the Habit Phase.

Chapter Recap

◆ A hallmark of the Sustained Action Phase is that we often don't want to do our resolution. This is the most challenging part of our journey, but each component of the Action-Ability Approach is designed to support your willingness.

◆ We need willingness to chug up two big hills: When we need to (1) use willpower to act on our resolution even if we don't want to and (2) use stillpower to direct ourselves away from an old unhealthy habit even when we have a strong urge to do it.

◆ One of the biggest obstacles to lasting change is the belief that we can perfectly design our Signs and Destinations so we always want to do the resolution.

◆ We can allow our conflicting thoughts, feelings and urges to be there, recognizing them as our biology in action. Notice the conflicting inner experience, exhale and redirect to the next two-minute action that keeps you on course.

◆ You can Urge Surf by using your stillpower to observe without action while the wave of emotion peaks and releases.

◆ We have only so much stamina for pushing ourselves forward. This needs to happen only occasionally.

◆ With repetition during the Sustained Action Phase, the inner experience eventually aligns with the new action. Then you know you've reached the Habit Phase.

Key Words

Willpower, Willingness, Want, Stillpower, Notice–Exhale–Redirect

Map Your Obstacle Course

From head to toe, Jamal is coated in mud. He scrambles up the ramped wall, quickly reaching up to grab Leah's outstretched hand. She and Adam hoist Jamal up over the barricade and onto the platform. Jamal turns around, extending his helping hand down to pull Alejandra up, keeping their team's momentum going. Before descending from this perch, Jamal catches a glimpse of the mud pit he just crawled through and turns to see the enormous net walls he and his coworkers will climb up and down next to get through this Tough Mudder obstacle course. Even Jamal's smile is muddy.

Creating a new habit requires each of us to navigate a personal obstacle course to get through the gritty Sustained Action Phase. Levels of difficulty vary. Jasmin breaking the absent-minded habit of biting her nails takes attention and effort, yet it's easier than the challenges faced by Rachel and Miranda as they learn to engage differently with anger or food. Marcus's path for speaking more with Kanesha was relatively easy but turned onto a steep hill when he needed to share about his father's death and talk with her about his intentions for his own healthcare.

At any difficulty level, the Action-Ability Approach enables us to map our unique obstacle course, empowering us to create lasting change. We can use the AAA Map below to summarize what we've learned so far and become nimbler at maneuvering through the remaining obstacles during the Sustained Action Phase.

The Action-Able Map

The triangle is a fitting shape for the AAA Map because it's the mathematical symbol for change. The steps inside the triangle build, one upon the next, to map our customized obstacle course. To create lasting change, we need:

- Compelling inspiration (Why)
- Understanding of the obstacles we face (Why Not)
- Plans for each obstacle (How)
- Social support for our plan (Who)
- Clarity about the very next step (What)
- Action (Do)

Using the AAA map, we gain clarity and strengthen our commitment. When we hit a barrier, we access our Action-Able Mindset to be compassionate, inquisitive and determined and seek support from our team to find a way forward for sustained action.

The Action-Ability Approach doesn't strategize about the goal. Instead, the planning focuses on the obstacles between us and our goal. We figure out how to get over, under, around or through the barriers to sustain our action.

Goal-oriented plans are different from obstacle-oriented plans. For example, if you want to be more organized, a goal-oriented plan could include "I will make a to-do list each morning of the tasks I need to complete today." This approach seems helpful, but it might not be related to why you're disorganized. Maybe you know what you need to do but struggle to transition between tasks. You get hyper-focused on what you're working on and lose track of time. Before you know it, you missed the timeframe for the phone call you were supposed to make. Even though the call is on your to-do list, you didn't get to it.

An obstacle-oriented plan addresses the challenge of hyper-focus. Knowing you get sucked in and lose track of time, you might set a loud alarm to disrupt yourself two minutes before you need to shift gears. The micro-action is to set the alarm before digging into the absorbing task. Plus, you may need a plan to actually stop when the alarm goes off. You decide to write a note to yourself about why the phone call is important. When the alarm goes off, you will remember the note and be more likely to pause and make the call.

AAA Maps illuminate obstacles along the path. When the obstacles are removed, the resolution is easy to do, like coasting downhill.

Miranda's breakthrough with eating healthier and keeping weight off came when she shifted from goal-oriented planning to the obstacle-oriented Action-Ability Approach. Rather than focusing on the goal of eating less, which left her grappling with an impossible list of don'ts, she learned about her obstacles, especially the What-the-Hell Effect. She worked with her KInD Coach and Manager to see and work around the Saboteur and the Tempted Self. She prepared her inner and outer environment to support her enjoyment of healthy cooking and eating.

I used to think my micromanaging was about parenting, but now I know anxiety is the real barrier to change. I am clear about my goal to stop nagging, but to be the parent I aspire to be, I need to find lots of ways to calm myself when I'm scared for my children. My Future Self reaches out a helping hand and hoists me over the obstacle of fear. I draw strength from the warm connection I have with my children and focus on the resilience we each possess. I exhale and call on my stillpower to stop speaking and find faith in my kids.

When-Then Action Planning

A powerful solution for living your best intentions is to create a step-by-step action plan using a when-then format.[1] *When* an obstacle presents, *then* you do a pre-planned action to move yourself forward.

For example, here is Rachel's When-Then Action Plan, summarizing what she's learned about how to calm herself when she's tired, edgy or irritable so she can be safe with Jason:

When (Obstacle)	Then (Plan)
When my resolution is framed negatively (Don't lash out at Jason)	then I translate *Don't* into *I will:* When I'm mad, I will exhale and walk away.
When struggling with an obsessive behavior	then I develop a substitute routine to do after the Stop Sign: When I'm edgy, I exhale and do my patience prayer.
When I'm confused about why I keep struggling with this	then I map out the detour Habit Pathway to see the challenge dynamic more clearly and map out the resolution Habit Pathway to see where I want to go at the crossroads.
When I miss the Stop Sign	then I connect with my KInD Coach and reflect back to learn more about what triggered my edginess. I incorporate what I learn to make Detour Alerts and Turn Signals to my Resolution Habit Pathway.
When I notice I'm irritable	then I exhale slowly and pray for patience with my beads in the morning and after work to keep my irritability as low as possible.

When (Obstacle)	Then (Plan)
When I notice I'm edgy	then I exhale and remind myself to "Be Nana, not Dad."
When I'm not sure how I'm feeling	then I pause and use my calm-agitated rating scale.
When I notice myself starting to pick a fight	then I exhale and use my willpower to turn and walk out of the room.
When I think I can't resist the urge to lash out	then I exhale, walk out of the room and emotionally vent (puke) in my journal.
When I think I can't resist the urge to lash out power	then I exhale, walk out of the room and tap into my still while using my mala beads to pray.
When I feel discouraged	then I connect with my KInD Coach, reminding myself that this habit can be changed and focus on why it's so important.
When I mess up and lash out	then I apologize to Jason and connect with my KInD Coach to learn what I missed so I can do it differently next time.
When I feel alone and discouraged	then I remind myself that Nana loves me no matter what.
When I'm edgy and want to lash out	then I go for a healthy relief reward so I can feel calmer *and* proud of myself.

When (Obstacle)	Then (Plan)
When I'm tired and not sure I can rally	then I remind myself of how much I love Jason and want our relationship to be close.

Each person's When-Then Action Plan is unique. Jamal's steps look nothing like Rachel's, Yolanda's or Tom's. My plan is different from yours.

Your When-Then Action Plan is just a list of your insights from completing the Action-Able Exercises. By writing out the steps for your obstacle course this way, you have clear directions for how to approach your unique situation. Also *when* you hit uncharted territory—an obstacle you didn't see coming—*then* you can shift to your pause-and-plan mode by slowing your breathing to call on your Manager, who can sort out how to proceed in the moment. Once you've gotten around the unforeseen obstacle, add your new insights to the chart.

Action-Able Exercise SA6:
Your When-Then Action Plan

Create a two-column table like Rachel's above: When (obstacle) / Then (plan). Based on what you've learned from reading and doing the other Action-Able Exercises, write out the obstacles you've discovered as well as your plans to overcome them. Also write down obstacles you're struggling with even if you aren't clear yet about how to overcome them.

> Appendix B uses the When-Then Action Planning format to give you a complete summary of the solutions you've learned in this book. It also specifies the Action-Able Exercises for handling each obstacle. Check out Appendix B to create plans for obstacles you're having a hard time with.
>
> Customize your When-Then Action Plan for your unique circumstances and personal tendencies.
>
> Add to your When-Then Action Plan as you learn more about what empowers you to succeed.

Your Customized Action-Able Map

Your When-Then Action Plan is like the street-level map offered by your GPS when you're following its turn-by-turn directions. It orients you to your Stop Signs, Detour Alerts and Turn Signals—"Rerouting. Rerouting."—and keeps you on course to your True Destination. Your GPS can also zoom out to show the overview map so you see the route in one glance. Similarly, you can create an Action-Able Map for your resolution to keep you oriented to the big picture during the Sustained Action Phase.

Use the Action-Able Map to create a handy Sign. Capture key ideas, words and phrases to summarize your insights.

For example, here is Rachel's personalized Action-Able Map for her resolution:

Rachel's Action-Able Map

Here is Tom's Action-Able Map:

Tom's Action-Able Map

As you can see, Rachel and Tom's Maps are totally different, each customized for their specific resolutions and unique circumstances, even though the Action-Ability Approach is always the same.

By customizing the Action-Able Map for your resolution, personality and situation, you create a helpful one-page summary of your key takeaways from this book.

Action-Able Exercise SA7:
Your customized Action-Able Map

Fill in your own Action-Able Map using key words and phrases summarizing what you've learned about how to create lasting change.

Color and decorate this image. Hang it in a noticeable place so it serves as a reminder of how to live your best intentions.

Chapter Recap

◆ Creating a new habit requires each of us to navigate
   a personal obstacle course to get through the
   challenging Sustained Action Phase.

◆ The Action-Ability Approach doesn't strategize
   about the goal. Instead, the planning focuses on
   the obstacles between us and our goal.

◆ Chart out a step-by-step action plan using a when-
   then format: *When* an obstacle presents, *then* you
   do a pre-planned action to move yourself forward.

◆ Design a customized Action-Able Map for your
   resolution, personality and situation for a helpful
   one-page summary of your key takeaways from
   this book.

Key Words

Obstacles, When-Then Action Plan, Action-Able Map

SUSTAINED ACTION PHASE
Action-Able Options

▶ Track your change process by observing your steps forward and back on the journey to becoming your Future Self.

▶ Anchor your pride in the process of *learning* from your successes and setbacks rather than over-focusing on goal behavior.

▶ Do a deeper analysis of what offers rewards for your unwanted habits and how to enhance the rewards for your resolution behavior. Increase your awareness of pleasant rewards that are physical, social, sensory and emotional, as well as of relief rewards.

▶ Develop new healthy relief rewards and use them to re-Fuel for sustained action.

▶ Map out your Reward Dilemma so you see the crossroads between your Detour Habit Pathway and your Resolution Habit Pathway.

▶ Create clear Detour Alerts and Turn Signals so you are reminded to take your resolution road when you get to the Stop Sign.

▶ Strengthen your willpower by doing a micro-action for your resolution even when you don't want to.

▶ Strengthen your stillpower by noticing conflicting thoughts, feelings and urges, exhaling and redirecting to sustained action for your resolution.

▶ Chart out a step-by-step action plan using a when-then format: *When* an obstacle presents, *then* you do a pre-planned action to move yourself forward.

▶ Update your action plan based on what you've learned during the Sustained Action Phase.

▶ Design a customized Action-Able Map for a helpful one-page summary of your key takeaways from this book.

Are any of these Action-Able steps relevant
to this moment in your journey?

Download the relevant exercise worksheets at
www.margithenderson.com/hope-to-habit-worksheets

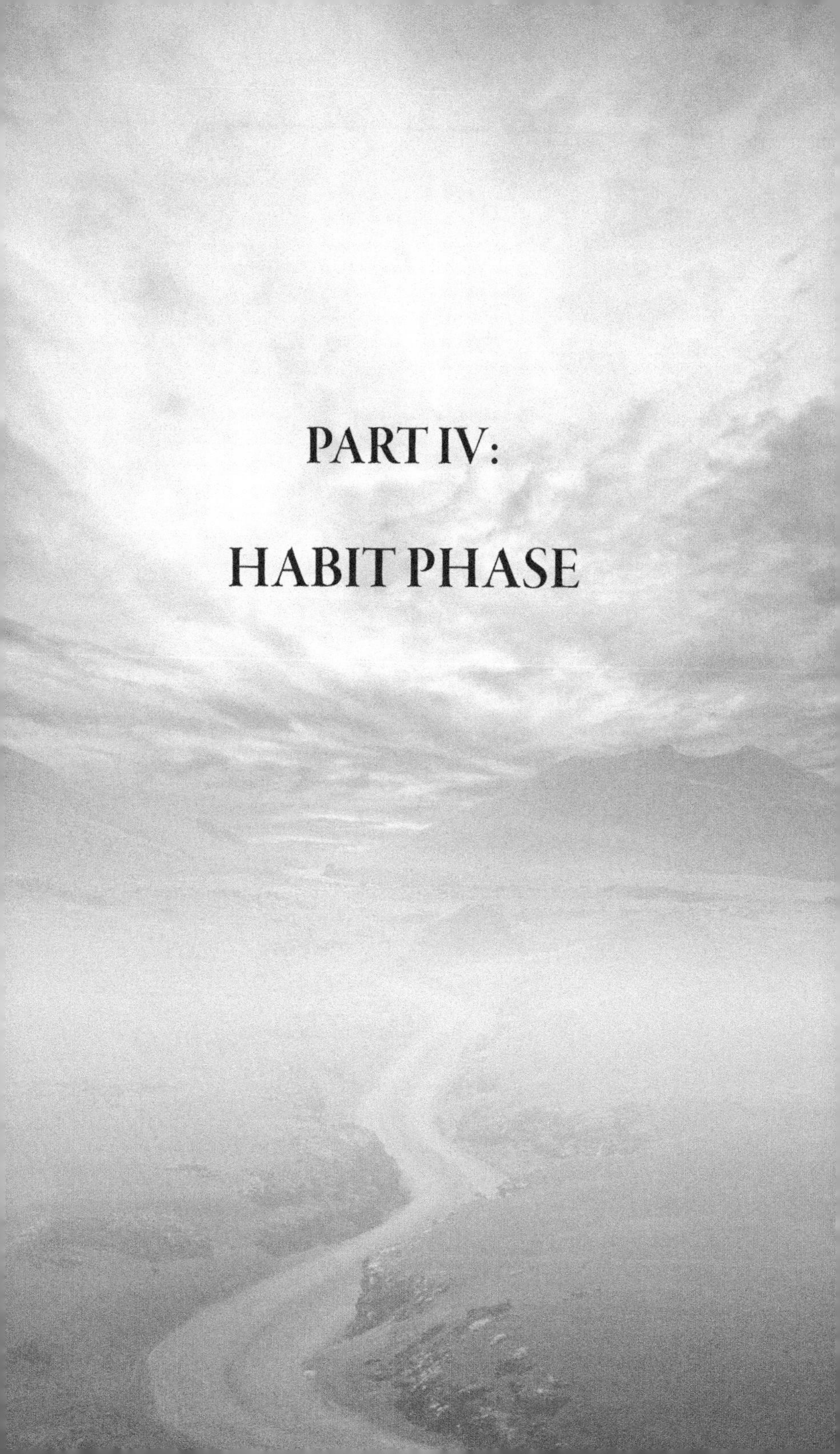

PART IV:

HABIT PHASE

The Hope of Habits

It's now June 2020 and my empty nest is full again. Because of the coronavirus pandemic, our adult children, whose college campuses closed, landed back home. Shocked by the sudden upending of our independent lives, we are "sheltering in place" together. You can see why I picked the goal to stop micromanaging—I don't want to make this hard situation worse. I'm committed to protecting the positive relationships I have with my kids by handling my anxiety differently and developing my stillpower.

Tom and Carol are among the multitude of Americans financially devastated by the economic impact of the coronavirus shutdown. At this point, one in four Americans are unemployed, countless businesses are on the brink of collapse, and the stock market is bucking wildly. People like Tom and Carol aren't to blame for the financial crisis they find themselves in, yet they must find a way forward. In different times, Tom and Carol might have returned to work, but now there are no jobs to be had. Instead, they're adjusting their expectations to manage with what they have, recognizing they're luckier than most.

Rachel prays for much more than patience these days. She leaves her beads in the car when she goes into the hospital for her nursing shift. Already more than 100,000 Americans have died of COVID-19 and nearly two million Americans have tested positive for the virus. The hospital is less chaotic after the first big wave of COVID-19 subsided. Today, Rachel is assigned to a non-COVID-19 floor for her shift. Though the hot breath caught in her mask is unpleasant, exhaling slowly calms her body down and helps her think more clearly under this pressure.

Jamal finally gets his wish. Working from home for the past three months, he's stopped counting his minutes on task because now his workdays flow with ease. He cranks on computer programming while his colleagues meet virtually without him.

Jasmin is relieved she broke her nail-biting habit when she did. Coronavirus spreads by people getting the virus on their hands and then touching their mouth, nose and eyes. Public health officials urge us to stop touching our faces, but we do it absent-mindedly. Jasmin's awareness helps her notice the subtle itch on her nose and use her stillpower to keep her hands away from her face.

Kanesha really struggles with the isolation of the stay-at-home order. She enjoys the video visits with her friends, but it's hard for someone so extroverted to be cooped up for months. She can't imagine her future without the big in-person gatherings she thrives on. Marcus doesn't mind the solitude, but he is heavy-hearted about what he sees on the television. Protesters have poured into the streets in most U.S. cities and are clashing with police and now the National

Guard. In the evenings, he listens and even chimes in as he and Kanesha talk, grappling with the unfolding events.

Yolanda welcomed Miranda, who was living alone and suddenly unemployed, to move in with her family when their city's stay-at-home order was issued. Miranda and Yolanda support each other during this anxious time, and the solidarity helps them avoid slipping back into old unhealthy habits. They cook together in the evenings.

During times of crisis like this, even well-established habits are easily upended—yet reclaiming our habits also gives us a path back to stability and calm.

Routines create a rhythm for our lives. When disrupted, as they are now, we feel out of sync and uneasy. Whether you're reading this during the coronavirus crisis or years into the future after life has settled into a new normal, look for ways to embrace habit and routine, savoring the comfort they add to your life.

Restoring habits resets our equilibrium. For example, during the pandemic, we're finding ways to re-create old habits using new technology, rebuilding the experiences and schedules to orient us. While it doesn't feel as good to congregate on video for our faith gatherings, it's reassuring to get back to weekly worship. Happy hour or game night with your friends might not be as much fun when done virtually, but it's a nice way to connect and frame your week. Structure and schedule can help us feel more settled.

Disruption is also a good time to break unwanted habits and create new ones.

New situations scramble the Signs for better or worse. For Jamal, working from home makes his life easier, and he's happy to hear from his supervisor that he's now permanently assigned to work from home. On the other hand, Miranda finds herself in a tougher situation at Yolanda's house with lots of junk food in reach, and yet she and Yolanda are able to contend with the temptation of the back shelf because they're doing it together.

Even positive events—such as getting married, moving, having a baby, starting a new job or retirement—change the Signs and can derail habits.

For big changes you can see coming, be proactive about the habits you want to keep and the ones you want to change. Create a When-Then Action Plan for your new situation, drawing on all you now know about creating habits.

Let's say you're starting a new job and want to prepare yourself better to make sure you don't get overwhelmed. You might set up your new work computer for better self-discipline. Knowing your tendency to overcommit, you block out timeframes on your calendar for each task so you see more clearly what your real availability is. You create folders for your new email account to better manage your incoming emails. The clean slate of your new job is easier to work with and sets you up for success.

You're a change expert now.

You understand how to use the Action-Ability Approach to develop a viable resolution, prepare your mental, social and physical environment and engage in sustained action to create the neural networks for your new habit. You know how to analyze Habit Pathways to transform an unwanted behavior into a habit you feel proud of by creating a customized AAA plan that works for your tendencies and circumstances.

You know how to decode the challenge dynamics of the habits you want to change. To change a behavior with an absent-minded dynamic, you'll track the action with KInD-ness, increasing your awareness of the Signs and Fuel. I used this solution to become aware of the bossy comments lurking in the corners of my mouth and now catch them more often before they slip out.

To stop obsessive behaviors, you'll find your stillpower to surf urges without acting on them and translate *Don't* into *I will* so you have a positive action to take instead. You'll create clear Detour Alerts to remind you of the negative outcomes of your unwanted habit and Turn Signals to send you in the right direction. Remember how Rachel, Miranda, Yolanda and I found unique paths to deal with our emotionally Fueled urges to yell, eat or nag.

To deal with an avoidant dynamic, you'll create rewards and determination to refill your willpower tank to Travel to your resolution. Your Future Self will inspire you to take action today. You'll find micro-actions that have big impacts, like Marcus's reflective listening that strengthened his connection with Kanesha.

You've learned how to make this less difficult by preparing yourself for success, like Tom removing his one-click buying option to slow down his absent-minded online shopping. You know how to re-Fuel with relief rewards so you can persist. Remember how Rachel uses prayer each day to strengthen her resolve or how Miranda and Yolanda draw on their friendship to cope with temptation and stay focused on health.

You've discovered the power of noticing the disruptive inner characters, thoughts, feelings and urges without fighting, then exhaling and redirecting your awareness to your resolution. You can stick with your resolution even when it's challenging, like Rachel did, pouring her anger into her journal rather than lashing out at Jason, or like Jamal and his willingness to risk conflict to remind his coworkers of the new plan.

Your Action-Able Mindset empowers you to quickly regroup from setbacks, calling on your compassion, curiosity and commitment. Recall how Miranda's KInD Coach disarmed the Inner Critic when they viewed him through the kaleidoscope. Or how Rachel's Future Self inspired her to use prayer beads to resist the Saboteur and find patience and calm, like her Nana. Or how Yolanda worked with her Manager to separate her snack items from her family's to improve her chances with the Tempted Self.

This is road construction work. With each repetition during the Sustained Action Phase, we create the neural networks that eventually become strong enough so we want to do our new action. When our thoughts, feelings and urges point us in the direction of our resolution, then we know our habit is fully formed.

My mind-my-own-business habit is still a work in progress. But my kids thank you for being my accountability partner on this resolution journey. They have seen me make progress, have setbacks and recommit, and they appreciate that I'm better than I was before.

My exercise habit was well established when I started writing to you, but it's taken some hits recently. I've had to find new ways to reward myself when my friend wasn't available. Plus, now our gym is closed due to the virus, so we'll have to find new strength training workouts. But these are just problems to be solved, and I know we can do it.

As I type these final words to you, after years of work and having wrestled with dozens of drafts, my writing habit is fully formed. Thank you for how you inspired me to persist, time and time again, keeping me going on this long journey with steep hills and spectacular views.

And now, as you take charge of your life by owning your habits, hear your KInD Coach, Future Self and me all cheering you on: "You can do this! Just take the very next step." Embrace the habit of hope.

Chapter Recap

◆ Routines create a rhythm for our lives. Look for ways to embrace habit and routine, savoring the comfort it adds to your life.

◆ Disruption can be a good time to break unwanted habits and create new ones.

◆ Even positive events—such as getting married, moving, having a baby, starting a new job or retirement—change the Signs and can derail established habits.

◆ For big changes you can see coming, be proactive about the habits you want to keep and the ones you want to change. Create a When-Then Action Plan for your new situation, drawing on all you now know about creating habits.

◆ You can do this! Embrace the habit of hope.

List of Action-Able Exercises

Sustained Action Phase   **Page #**

Chapter/Exercise #

Appendix A:
Feeling Words

Joyful
Happy
Delighted
Excited
Enthusiastic
Inspired
Passionate
Playful
Thrilled
Refreshed
Hopeful
Energized

Calm
Content
Present
Fulfilled
Peaceful
Patient
Relaxed

Loving
Caring
Compassionate
Accepting
Affectionate
Safe
Connected
Tender
Warm

Appreciative
Grateful
Fortunate
Thankful
Lucky

Courageous
Powerful
Brave
Capable
Daring
Determined
Strong
Solid
Empowered

Curious
Intrigued
Fascinated
Interested
Engaged

Numb
Flat
Apathetic
Bored
Withdrawn
Shut down
Distant
Indifferent

Anxious
Fearful
Afraid
Apprehensive
Frightened
Nervous
Scared
Terrified
Worried

Sad
Disappointed
Depressed
Despondent
Bereft
Hopeless
Unhappy
Melancholy

Lonely
Heartbroken
Forlorn
Longing
Envious
Disconnected

Tired
Weary
Fatigued
Exhausted
Depleted
Listless
Lethargic
Worn out
Burdened

Stressed
Frazzled
Overwhelmed
Tense
Burned out
Edgy

Guilty
Regret
Sorry
Remorseful

Angry
Irritated
Agitated
Frustrated
Impatient
Edgy
Aggravated
Resentful
Vindictive
Enraged
Defensive
Hostile

Ashamed
Embarrassed
Self-conscious
Humiliated
Mortified

Powerless
Helpless
Fragile
Trapped
Impotent
Vulnerable

Confused
Unsettled
Doubtful
Disturbed
Unsure
Hesitant
Uneasy

Body Sensation Words

Warm	Expansive	Dizzy	Constricted
Tingling	Light	Frozen	Achy
Tender	Gentle	Hollow	Buzzy
Spacious	Calm	Tense	Jumpy
Soft	Still	Tight	Pounding
Relaxed	Spacey	Trembling	Queasy
Radiating	Empty	Rigid	Throbbing
Electric	Numb	Knotted	Burning
Full	Blocked	Clenched	

Appendix B:

When-Then Action Plan
Recap

The insights from this book are mapped out below using the When-Then Action Planning structure. This table serves as a handy overview of what you've learned.

WHEN	THEN (Exercise #)
RESOLUTION PHASE	
When I am tempted to make a resolution to get relief from feeling guilt or shame (False Hope Syndrome)	then I will redirect myself to saying, "I can" or "I want to change because" (R1) and I will develop my healthy relief rewards (SA2) to cope with these feelings.
When I'm unclear about how to approach my resolution	then I will clarify my change challenge to see the absent-minded, obsessive or avoidant dynamics (R2).
When I'm unclear about how to approach my resolution	then I will map the Habit Pathway to see my change challenge more clearly (SA3).
When I'm focused on a habit I want to stop doing	then I will plan a substitute action, translating *Don't* into *I will*, and redirect my focus on what I will do instead (R3, SA3).
When I want to change an absent-minded behavior	then I will focus on discovering the Signs for the absent-minded action (P4, P8) and make Turn Signals to point to the substitute action (P3, P16, SA3, SA7).

WHEN	THEN (Exercise #)
RESOLUTION PHASE	
When I want to change an obsessive behavior	then I will build my stillpower (SA4) and Notice–Exhale(R4)–Redirect to the new behavior (P16, SA3) and healthy relief rewards (SA2).
When I want to change an avoidant behavior	then I will re-**Fuel** by clarifying my why (P5), connecting with my Future Self (P11, P12) and refreshing my energy to persist (SA2).
When I made a big resolution that is hard to stick with	then I will create micro-resolutions to make my goal more approachable (P16).
When I feel unsure if I can do the work to make my resolution a habit	then I will re-**Fuel** (SA2) and focus on the rewards of my new habit (P5, P12).
When I feel discouraged and want to give up after a setback	then I will Notice–Exhale–Redirect my awareness to the KInD Coach (P2, P6).
PREPARATION PHASE	
When I'm being harsh with myself after a setback	then I will notice my Inner Critic (P1), exhale and redirect to my KInD Coach (P2, P6) and focus on compassion.
When I think that inner reprimands and stern restrictions are the only way to keep myself on track	then I will remind myself these approaches activate the What-the-Hell Effect, and redirect to my KInD Coach (P2, P6).

WHEN	THEN (Exercise #)
PREPARATION PHASE	
When I don't understand why I had a setback	then I will be inquisitive and search for the obstacle in my path (P4, P14).
When I lose hope that I can change	then I will re-Fuel my determination by focusing on why my resolution is important (P5, P11, P12).
When I don't feel supported by my family and friends for the habit I'm working on	then I will orient to the positive people in my life and find new relationships with KInD people (P7).
When I have a strong craving for an obsessive behavior	then I will notice my Tempted Self (P8), exhale (R4), use my stillpower (SA5) and redirect to focus on my Manager (P9) and KInD Coach (P2, P6).
When I start to rationalize a lapse (Halo Effect) or say "What the hell!" and feel myself getting ready to give up on my resolution	then I will notice the Saboteur (P10) and Tempted Self (P8), exhale (R4) and redirect to the KInD Coach (P2, P6), Manager (P9) and Future Self (P11). I will be aware that the Saboteur can seem nice, disguised as the KInD Coach.
When I feel depleted	then I will use treats and healthy relief rewards (SA2) to re-Fuel.

WHEN	THEN (Exercise #)
PREPARATION PHASE	
When the Saboteur says change should happen quickly and easily	then I will remind myself of the brain science showing that it takes a while for the new neural network to be established. I will orient to the KInD Coach (P2, P6) and the positive people in my life (P7), focus on why my goal is important (P5, P12), re-Fuel with a relief reward (SA2) and develop micro-actions (P16) so I feel up to the challenging path.
When the Saboteur is using the Future Self to push-off change or justify a last hurrah	then I will notice, exhale (R4) and redirect to the KInD Coach (P6) to take a micro-action now (P16) and focus on gratitude from my Future Self (P12) to help me take action today.
When I can't find the items that set me up for success	then I will prepare my environment to have the needed supplies in the right place, at the right time (P16).
When I am surrounded by temptation	then I will remove tempting items from my environment and get the right supplies set up where I need them (P16).
When I forget to do my goal action	then I will create Signs to remind me to do my new behavior (P16, SA3, SA7).

WHEN	THEN (Exercise #)
PREPARATION PHASE	
When I'm trying a one-size-fits-all solution and I feel discouraged	then I will customize my approach with the Hero's tendencies and circumstances in mind (P14, P16, SA6).
SUSTAINTED ACTION PHASE	
When I'm struggling with my resolution and the old unwanted habit is still strong	then I will call on my KInD Coach (P2, P6) to remind me I need to repeat my new action over and over to create the neural networks for my resolution habit.
When I lack awareness about my resolution action	then I will track change by counting steps forward and back, being inquisitive about how successes and setbacks happen (SA1).
When the Inner Critic and Saboteur try to weaponize tracking, focusing my thinking on good/bad, right/wrong, success/failure and pushing me toward the Pride-Shame Loop	then I will notice, exhale (R4) and redirect to tracking by the KInD Coach (P2, P6) who approaches setbacks as learning experiences (SA1).
When the Saboteur tries to use tracking to turn progress against me (Halo Effect)	then I will notice, exhale (R4) and redirect to the KInD Coach (P6) and focus on pride in the process, not the outcome (SA1).

WHEN	THEN (Exercise #)
SUSTAINED ACTION PHASE	
When the Saboteur discourages tracking	then I will notice, exhale (R4) and redirect to the importance of tracking for developing awareness, the linchpin for change (SA1).
When I think that I need to wait until my emotions and thoughts point to my resolution, to wait until I want to do it	then I will remind myself to take steps today to become my Future Self (P11), to act how I want to feel, and focus on gratitude from the future (P12).
When I notice my willpower is exhausted	then I will exhale (R4), re-Fuel using relief rewards (SA2) and prepare the environment for success (P16).
When I lack awareness about what rewards my habits	then I will be inquisitive and discover the pleasant and relief rewards driving my behavior and map out my Reward Dilemma (SA3).
When I notice that relief rewards drive my detour Habit Pathway	then I will develop healthy relief rewards to use as substitute actions (SA2, SA3).
When I have trouble making the turn away from the Detour onto the Resolution Habit Pathway	I will create a Stop Sign, Detour Alert and Turn Signal to make sure I notice the crossroads and make the turn to my resolution road.
When I think I should always want to do my resolution action	then I will discover my willingness to act even when I don't want to (SA5).

WHEN	THEN (Exercise #)
SUSTAINED ACTION PHASE	
When I think I cannot resist a powerful urge	then I will discover my then I will discover my still-power (SA5) and redirect to my healthy relief rewards (SA2) and resolution action (SA3) while the urge passes.
When I hit a setback with a previously invisible obstacle	then I will be inquisitive about this obstacle and develop a plan to address it (SA6).
When I feel overwhelmed by all I've learned in this book	then I will create a When-Then Action Plan of my insights to clarify and consolidate my learning (SA6).
When I need a reminder of my action plan	then I will create my custom-ized Action-Able Map for a one-page overview of my action plan (SA7).

Recommended Reading

Clear, James. *Atomic Habits: An Easy and Proven Way to Build Good Habits and Break Bad Ones.* London, UK: Penguin Random House, 2018.

Dawson, Peg, and Richard Guare. *The Smart but Scattered Guide to Success: How to Use Your Brain's Executive Skills to Keep Up, Stay Calm and Get Organized at Work and at Home.* New York: Guilford Press, 2016.

Dean, Jeremy. *Making Habits, Breaking Habits: Why We Do Things, Why We Don't, and How to Make Any Change Stick.* Boston: De Capo Press, 2013.

Duhigg, Charles. *The Power of Habit: Why We Do What We Do in Life and Business.* New York: Random House, 2012.

Dweck, Carol S. *Mindset: The New Psychology of Success.* New York: Random House, 2006.

McGonigal, Kelly. *The Willpower Instinct: How Self-Control Works, Why It Matters, and What You Can Do to Get More of It.* New York: Penguin Group, 2012.

Neff, Kristin. *Self-Compassion: The Proven Power of Being Kind to Yourself.* New York: William Morrow HarperCollins, 2011.

Prochaska, James, Norcross, John, and Carlo DiClemente. *Changing for Good: A Revolutionary Six-Stage Program for Overcoming Bad Habits and Moving Your Life Positively Forward.* New York: HarperCollins, 1994.

Rubin, Gretchen. *Better than Before: What I Learned about Making and Breaking Habits—to Sleep More, Quit Sugar, Procrastinate Less, and Generally Build a Happier Life.* New York: Broadway Books, 2015.

Thaler, Richard, and Cass Sunstein. *Nudge: Improving Decisions about Health, Wealth, and Happiness.* New Haven: Yale University Press, 2008.

Young, Sean. *Stick with It: A Scientifically Proven Process for Changing Your Life-for Good.* New York: Harper Collins, 2017.

Notes

Chapter 2: The Challenging Path to Change

[1] Mostly I've drawn from research in neuroscience and health psychology regarding intention implementation; for example, see Gollwitzer, P. M., & Sheeran, P. (2006). Implementation intentions and goal achievement: A meta-analysis of effects and processes. *Advances in Experimental Social Psychology*, 38, 69–119.

[2] From W.C. Fields 1938 performance of his comedic radio monologue "The Temperance Lecture." Quote confirmed by Shapiro, F (2006). T*he Yale book of quotations.* New Haven: Yale University Press, p. 256.

[3] Another model explaining the stages of change is described by Prochaska, J. O., Norcross, J. C., & DiClemente, C. C. (1994). *Changing for good: A revolutionary six-stage program for overcoming bad habits and moving your life positively forward.* New York: HarperCollins.

[4] Sprake, C. (2017, March). *Heart of an eight-figure business.* Keynote speech presented at the National Speakers Association annual conference, Orlando, FL.

Chapter 3: Promises, Promises

[1] The habit loop (cue-routine-reward) is described by Duhigg, C. (2012). *The power of habit: Why we do what we do in life and business.* New York: Random House.

[2] The role of craving in creating habits is further elaborated by Clear, J. (2018). *Atomic habits: An easy and proven way to build good habits and break bad ones.* London, UK: Penguin Random House.

[3] Polivy, J., & Herman, C. P. (2002). If at first you don't succeed: False hopes of self-change. *American Psychologist*, 57, 677–89.

Chapter 4: Clarifying Your Resolution Challenge

[1] Young, S. (2017). *Stick with it: A scientifically proven process for changing your life–for good.* New York: Harper Collins. Young describes his ABCs of behavior classification—behaviors are either automatic (absent-minded), burning (obsessive) or common (which can be absent-minded or avoidant).

Chapter 5: Don't Don't

[1] Dean, J. (2013). *Making habits, breaking habits: Why we do things, why we don't, and how to make any change stick.* Boston: De Capo Press, p. 160.   .
[2] Polivy, J., & Herman, C. P. (1985). Dieting and binging: A causal analysis. *American Psychologist*, 40, 193–201. Also Polivy, J., Herman, C. P., & Deo, R. (2010). Getting a bigger slice of the pie. Effects on eating and emotion in restrained and unrestrained eaters. *Appetite*, 55, 426-30.

Chapter 6: Micro-Resolutions

[1] For a further discussion of the research and power of breathing practices, see Nestor, J. (2020). *Breath: The new science of a lost art.* New York: Riverhead.
[2] Segerstrom, S. C., Hardy, J. K., Evans, D. R., & Winters, N. F. (2012). Pause and plan: Self-regulation and the heart. In Wrights, R. A., & Gendolla, G. H. E. (Eds.). *How motivation affects cardiovascular response: Mechanisms and*

applications. (pp. 181–198). Washington, DC: American Psychological Association.

Chapter 8: Action-Able Mindset

[1] Kolata, G. (2016, May 2). After 'The Biggest Loser,' their bodies fought to regain weight. The New York Times. https://www.nytimes.com/2016/05/02/health/biggest-loser-weight-loss.html

[2] Duckworth, A. (2016). *Grit: The power of passion and perseverance.* New York: Scribner.

[3] McGonigal, K. (2012). *The willpower instinct: How self-control works, why it matters, and what you can do to get more of it.* New York: Penguin Group.

[4] Trumpeter, N., Watson, P. J., & O'Leary, B. J. (2006). Factors within multidimensional perfectionism scales: Complexity of relationships with self-esteem, narcissism, self-control, and self-criticism. *Personality and Individual Differences, 41,* 849–60.

[5] This is referred to as Metacognition, see Chapter 7 in Dawson, P., & Guare, R. (2016). *The smart but scattered guide to success: How to use your brain's executive skills to keep up, stay calm and get organized at work and at home.* New York: Guilford Press.

[6] This approach comes from Narrative Therapy. See Morgan, A. (2000). *What is Narrative Therapy? An easy-to-read introduction.* Adeliaide, South Africa: Dulwich Centre.

[7] Neff, K. (2011). *Self-compassion: The proven power of being kind to yourself.* New York: William Morrow HarperCollins.

[8] Leary, M. R., Tate, E. B., Adams, C. E., Allen, A. B., & Hancock, J. (2007). Self-compassion and reactions to unpleasant self-relevant events: The implications of treating

oneself kindly. *Journal of Personality and Social Psychology*, 92, 887–904. See also Chamberlin, J. M., & Haaga, D. A. F. (2001). Unconditional self-acceptance and responses to negative feedback. *Journal of Rational-Emotive & Cognitive-Behavioral Therapy*, 19, 177–89.

[9] The importance of mindset is described by Carol Dweck whose research illuminates the difference between a Fixed Mindset and a Growth Mindset, see Dweck, C. S. (2006). *Mindset: The new psychology of success.* New York: Random House.

[10] McGonigal, K. (2012). T*he willpower instinct: How self-control works, why it matters, and what you can do to get more of it.* New York: Penguin Group, p. 237.

[11] This line of questioning comes from Solution-Focused Brief Therapy (SFBT) practice of seeking and exploring exceptions to the problem. See deShazer, S., & Dolan, Y. with Korman, H., Trepper, T., McCollum, E., & Kim Berg, I. (2007). *More Than miracles: The state of the art of Solution-Focused Brief Therapy.* New York: Haworth.

[12] Duhigg, C. (2012). T*he power of habit: Why we do what we do in life and business.* New York: Random House, p. 20.

[13] This is referred to as Goal-Directed Persistence, see Chapter 18 in Dawson, P., & Guare, R. (2016). *The smart but scattered guide to success: How to use your brain's executive skills to keep up, stay calm and get organized at work and at home.* New York: Guilford Press.

[14] This is approach comes from Narrative Therapy and is called Externalization, for example see Morgan, A. (2000). *What is Narrative Therapy? An easy-to-read introduction.* Adeliaide, South Africa: Dulwich Centre. The idea of handling challenging inner parts is also well developed in Acceptance Commitment Therapy, known as ACT and

described in Hayes, S. C. (2005). *Get out of your mind and into your life: The new Acceptance and Commitment Therapy (A New Harbinger self-help workbook).* Oakland, CA: New Harbinger.

[15] Regarding Keystone Habits, see Chapter 4 in Duhigg, C. (2012). *The power of habit: Why we do what we do in life and business.* New York: Random House.

Chapter 9: Your Cast of Characters

[1] Regarding Community, see Chapter 3 in Young, S. (2017). *Stick with it: A scientifically proven process for changing your life–for good.* New York: Harper Collins.

[2] The Framingham studies are the most powerful examples of this social contagion phenomenon. See Christakis, N. A., & Fowler, J. H. (2007). The spread of obesity in a large social network over 32 years. *New England Journal of Medicine,* 357, 370–79. Also, Christakis, N. A., & Fowler, J. H. (2008). The collective dynamics of smoking in a large social network. *New England Journal of Medicine,* 358, 2249–58.

[3] Clear, J. (2018). *Atomic habits: An easy and proven way to build good habits and break bad ones.* London, UK: Penguin Random House, p. 94.

[4] McGonigal, K. (2012). *The willpower instinct: How self-control works, why it matters, and what you can do to get more of it.* New York: Penguin Group, p. 17.

[5] Dawson, P., & Guare, R. (2016). *The smart but scattered guide to success: How to use your brain's executive skills to keep up, stay calm and get organized at work and at home.* New York: Guilford Press.

[6] Segerstrom, S.C., & Nes, L. S. (2007). Heart rate variability reflects self-regulatory strength, effort and fatigue. *Psychological Science,* 18, 275–81. Also, Thayer, J. F., Hansen, A. L.,

Saus-Rose, E., & Johnsen, B. H. (2009). Heart rate variability, prefrontal neural function, and cognitive performance: The neurovisceral integration perspective on self-regulation, adaptation, and health. *Annals of Behavioral Medicine*, 37, 141–53.

[7] This is referred to as Moral Licensing, see Monin, B., & Miller, D. T. (2001). Moral credentials and the expression of prejudice. *Journal of Personality and Social Psychology*, 81, 33–43. Also, Sachdeva, S., Iliev, R., & Medin, D. L. (2009). Sinning saints and saintly sinners: The paradox of moral self-regulation. *Psychological Science*, 20, 523–28.

[8] Chandon, P., & Wansink, B. (2007). The biasing health halos of fast-food restaurant health claims: Lower calorie estimates and higher side-dish consumption intentions. *Journal of Consumer Research*, 34, 301–14. Also, Chernev, A. (2011). The dieter's paradox. *Journal of Consumer Psychology*, 21, 178–83.

[9] Regarding Treats, see Just Because chapter, pg. 201, in Rubin, G. (2015). *Better than before: What I learned about making and breaking habits—to sleep more, quit sugar, procrastinate less, and generally build a happier life.* New York: Broadway Books.

[10] This is referred to as Goal Liberation, see Fishback, A., & Dhar, R. (2005). Goals as excuses or guides: The liberating effect of perceived goal progress on choice. *Journal of Consumer Research*, 32, 370–77.

[11] This is referred to as Future Self Continuity, see Murru, E.C., & Martin Ginis, K. A. (2010). Imagining the possibilities: The effects of a possible selves intervention on self-regulatory efficacy and exercise behavior. *Journal of Sport & Exercise Psychology*, 32, 537–54.

[12] Ersner-Hershfield, H., Goldstein, D. G., Sharpe, W. F., Fox, J., Yeykelis, L., Carstensen, L.L., & Bailenson J. (2011). Increasing saving behavior through age-progressed renderings of the future self. *Journal of Marketing Research*, 48, 23–37. See also, Ersner-Hershfield, H., Garton, M.T., Ballard, K., Samanez-Larkin, G. R., & Knutson, B. (2009). Don't stop thinking about tomorrow: Individual differences in future self-continuity account for saving. *Judgment and Decision Making*, 4, 280–86.

[13] Rubin, G. (2015). *Better than before: What I learned about making and breaking habits—to sleep more, quit sugar, procrastinate less, and generally build a happier life.* New York: Broadway Books, p. 63.

[14] For more about how behavior change precedes emotional and cognitive change, see Chapter 6 regarding Neurohacks in Young, S. (2017). *Stick with it: A scientifically proven process for changing your life—for good.* New York: Harper Collins.

[15] This question comes from Solution-Focused Brief Therapy, known as the Miracle Question. See deShazer, S., & Dolan, Y., with Korman, H., Trepper, T., McCollum, E., & Kim Berg, I. (2007). *More than miracles: The state of the art of Solution-Focused Brief Therapy.* New York: Haworth.

[16] See Neurohacks chapter in Young, S. (2017). *Stick with it: A scientifically proven process for changing your life—for good.* New York: Harper Collins.

[17] Clear, J. (2018). *Atomic habits: An easy and proven way to build good habits and break bad ones.* London, UK: Penguin Random House, p. 38.

[18] Clear, J. (2018). *Atomic habits: An easy and proven way to build good habits and break bad ones.* London, UK: Penguin Random House, p. 37.

Chapter 10: You Are the Hero

[1] An intriguing discussion of individual differences in habit formation is offered by Rubin, G. (2015). *Better than before: What I learned about making and breaking habits—to sleep more, quit sugar, procrastinate less, and generally build a happier life.* New York: Broadway Books. Her ideas about personal tendencies in response to expectations (classifying people as upholders, questioners, obligers and rebels) don't have research support yet but are thought-provoking and illuminating.

[2] Duhigg, C. (2012). *The power of habit: Why we do what we do in life and business.* New York: Random House.

Chapter 11: Set the Stage for Change

[1] Baumeister, R. F., Heatherton, T. F., & Tice, D. M. (1994). *Losing control: How and why people fail at self-regulation.* San Diego: Academic Press. Also, Vohs, K. D., Baumeister, R. F., Schmeichel, B. J., Twenge, J. M., Nelson, N. M., & Tice, D. M. (2008). Making choices impairs subsequent self-control: A limited-resources account of decision making, self-regulation, and active initiative. *Journal of Personality and Social Psychology*, 94, 883–98.

[2] McGonigal, K. (2012). *The willpower instinct: How self-control works, why it matters, and what you can do to get more of it.* New York: Penguin Group, p.14.

[3] Thaler, R.H., & Sunstein, C. R. (2008). *Nudge: Improving decisions about health, wealth, and happiness.* New Haven: Yale University Press.

[4] The Bullitt Center: Irresistible Stairs: https://bullittcenter.org/building/building-features/active-design/

[5] de Vries, H., Eggers, S. E., & Bolman, C. (2013). The role of action planning and plan enactment for smoking cessation. *BMC Public Health*, 13, 393.

[6] See Habit Stacking in Clear, J. (2018). *Atomic habits: An easy and proven way to build good habits and break bad ones*. London, UK: Penguin Random House, p. 72.

[7] The Golden Rule of Habit Change is described in Chapter 3 of Duhigg, C. (2012). *The power of habit: Why we do what we do in life and business*. New York: Random House.

[8] Gollwitzer, P. M., & Sheeran, P. (2006). Implementation intentions and goal achievement: A meta-analysis of effects and processes. *Advances in Experimental Social Psychology*, 38, 69–119.

Chapter 12: Persistence

[1] Hebb, D. (1949). *The organization of behavior: A neuropsychological theory*. New York: Wiley, p. 62. Concept by Hebb, wording by Carla Shatz.

[2] See chapter on Engrained in Young, S. (2017). *Stick with it: A scientifically proven process for changing your life – for good*. New York: Harper Collins.

[3] Clear, J. (2018). *Atomic habits: An easy and proven way to build good habits and break bad ones*. London, UK: Penguin Random House, p. 146.

[4] Smith, D., & Bolam, J. P. (1990). The neural network of the basal ganglia as revealed by the study of synaptic connections of identified neurones. *Trends in Neuroscience*, 13, 259-65.

Chapter 13: Tracking Change

[1] In Proverbs 16:18, *Holy Bible (Revised Standard Version)*

warns "Pride goes before destruction, a haughty spirit before a fall." Old Testament, p. 571

[2] James Clear shared a version of this idea, which inspired my paperclips chain, in his book, Clear, J. (2018). *Atomic habits: An easy and proven way to build good habits and break bad ones.* London, UK: Penguin Random House.

Chapter 14: The Reward Dilemma

[1] Duhigg, C. (2012). *The power of habit: Why we do what we do in life and business.* New York: Random House.

[2] See chapter on Captivating in Young, S. (2017). *Stick with it: A scientifically proven process for changing your life – for good.* New York: Harper Collins.

[3] McGonigal, K. (2015). *The upside of stress: Why stress is good for you, and how to get good at it.* New York: Penguin Random House.

[4] For more calming breathing strategies, see Nestor, J. (2020). *Breath: The new science of a lost art.* New York:

[5] Pychyl, T. (2013). *Solving the procrastination puzzle: A concise guide to strategies for change.* New York: Penguin Random House.

[6] Duhigg, C. (2012). *The power of habit: Why we do what we do in life and business.* New York: Random House, p. 63. Riverhead.

Chapter 15: Willpower and Stillpower

[1] Kelly McGonigal describes the ideas of will-power and won't-power in her book, McGonigal, K. (2012). *The will-power instinct: How self-control works, why it matters, and what you can do to get more of it.* New York: Avery Penguin Group, p. 14.

[2] The idea of driving a vehicle while coping with challenging inner parts comes from Acceptance Commitment Therapy, known as ACT. See Hayes, S. C. (2005). *Get out of your mind and into your life: The new Acceptance and Commitment Therapy (A New Harbinger self-help workbook).* Oakland, CA: New Harbinger.

[3] Duhigg, C. (2012). *The power of habit: Why we do what we do in life and business.* New York: Random House, p. 68.

[4] Griffin, K. (2010, Spring). Interview with G. Alan Marlatt: *Surfing the Urge, Inquiring Mind,* 26(2). https://www.inquiringmind.com/article/2602_w_marlatt-interview-with-g-alan-marlatt-surfing-the-urge/

Chapter 16: Map Your Obstacle Course

[1] This is referred to as If-Then Planning; see Gollwitzer, P. M., & Sheeran, P. (2006). Implementation intentions and goal achievement: A meta-analysis of effects and processes. *Advances in Experimental Social Psychology,* 38, 69–119.

Acknowledgments

This book is the culmination of much of what I've learned about creating lasting change over my 30-plus-year career as a psychologist. My greatest teachers have been the clients in my clinical practice. While I could not share your confidential stories here, you have inspired me and deepened my understanding of how change happens. I am a better psychologist and a healthier person because of you.

My heartfelt thanks goes to the colleagues and friends who came to workshops where I tried to wrestle these concepts into a workable process and who read early drafts of this book. You helped immensely to clarify and enrich this book and the Action-Ability Approach: Daniela Abbott, Laura Braafladt, Gretl Cox, Christy Cutler, Susan Daggett, Terri Davis, Beth Doyle, Gillian Egan, Sarah Hower, Letticia Kratz, Marla Rodriguez, Dan and Julie Schlager, Bill Walters and Gigi Willett. Thanks especially to Lee Massaro—you transformed this book. You were my KInD Coach, firmly pushing me to learn how to use storytelling to bring the Action-Able concepts to life in these pages.

Thank you to Susan Daggett for coming up with the book's title and to Marla Rodriguez for bringing me back to the title and helping me sort out the subtitle. Thanks to Gigi Willett for your illustration of the Habit Pathway and to Paul Vorreiter for designing the Action-Able Map. Thank you Terri Davis for the idea of making the downloadable workbook and worksheets. I am grateful to Craig Lancaster of Lancarello

Enterprises for copyediting and to Nick Zelinger of NZ Graphics for the cover design and book layout. Thanks also to Neen James, whose National Speakers Association 2017 annual conference workshop on creating visual models sparked my creation of the Action-Ability Approach triangle model, which lit the fire in me to write this book.

Finally, I am deeply grateful to my husband, Stalker Henderson, and children, Theo and Caity. Your loving encouragement sustained me during my years of labor on this project. You are my beacons of hope. You inspire me to live my best intentions.

About the Author

As a therapist, speaker and writer, Dr. Margit Cox Henderson is an Action-Ability catalyst. She draws on almost 30 years of experience as a clinical and health psychologist, sharing her research-based understanding about behavior change to lengthen healthspan and activate joyful living.

As a therapist, Margit has been in private practice for 20-plus years. Previously, she worked in community mental health and college counseling. She has been a professional speaker throughout her career, teaching undergraduate and graduate students, as well as presenting at professional conferences and community events. Margit's work has been published in professional research journals, and her first book, *Optimistic Aging*, was published in 2014 and won the Independent Publisher's 2015 Living Now Book Award.

Margit lives in Denver, Colorado. She has been happily married for nearly 30 years and has two adult children who keep her challenged, inspired and delighted. Margit enjoys spending time with her family and friends, skiing and hiking in the beautiful Colorado mountains and taking long walks with her squirrel-obsessed dog, especially when someone else is holding the leash.

For more information and to contact Margit with your reactions, questions and input, visit:

www.margithenderson.com

or email her at margit@margithenderson.com.

Made in the USA
Coppell, TX
05 January 2021